Praise for The Conscious Classroom

"Amy Edelstein's The Conscious Classroom *is a must read for anyone interested in where the world is going, how to transform education and what to do to elevate human behavior. Forty-two percent of the world's population is twenty-five years old and younger. Amy's Inner Strength System™ offers teens all around the world a compass to gain inner peace, find their unique purpose, and motivate them to serve others."*

—Sam Beard,
founder and president GIFT, founder of the Jefferson Awards,
America's Nobel Prize for Service with Jacqueline
Kennedy Onassis and Senator Robert Taft, Jr.

"At a time when discussions about the meaning and purpose of education in the United States are stuck in ideological debates rather than imaginative conversations, Amy Edelstein offers a way through the quagmire. She calls for an 'education of emergence' that combines a clear-eyed, honest understanding of the realities of classroom teaching and the demands of 'standards-based' learning, with a deep commitment to mindful pedagogies that enable students to develop more insightful, subtle, inclusive, and systemic ways of seeing. Edelstein explains why a conscious classroom matters and provides specific methodology for how to make it happen in our own teaching. A game changer, this book defines the path for how we might collaborate to fulfill the mission of educating conscious citizens."

—Jonathan Miller-Lane, Ph.D.
Director, Program in Education Studies,
Middlebury College, VT

"The Conscious Classroom *provides a model for both educators and students to be empowered by cultivating the inner resources of strength, resilience, and compassion that support stability in the midst of life's challenges. Through stories of her own and those of her students, Amy Edelstein skillfully shows us the power of mindful awareness in developing clarity, perspective, and inner stability in teens and teachers. She also shows and how these benefits can ripple out far and wide. This is an inspiring book that looks towards the future with open possibility and with the potential for goodness and well-being to prevail in our youth, our schools, and our communities."*

—Diane Reibel, Ph.D.,
director, Mindfulness Institute, Mryna Brind
Center of Integrative Medicine, Thomas Jefferson
University, co-author of *Teaching Mindfulness: A practical guide for clinicians and educators*

"Amy Edelstein's work, of which she gives us a taste in this book, invites us all to trust what we know about human beings, even the teen-aged ones. When they are supported and inspired, trusted and respected as persons, they will be creative and insightful makers of the change we need in the world. The idea that time and space to meditate might be the core of what high schools need challenges the rigid thinking that too often prevails in education. Amy makes it vivid with stories of students' insights, teachers' lessons and accessible explanations of the kinds of exciting ideas and attitudes toward which students are led. To be able to manage reactions, see things from different perspectives, and place things in the largest possible context, these are the gifts students take and apply to the almost unimaginable obstacles they face. I left this book with more hope for the world the next generation will create than I have had in a long time."

—Eric Hoffman, Ph.D.,
St. Joseph University, conductor Essentials Experience,
former director of American Philosophical Association

"In our troubled times, this is the book educators, teens, and other concerned beings have waited for. In The Conscious Classroom, *Amy Edelstein, with love and wisdom, takes all her readers by the hand, leads them to the edge of the abyss, and gives them wings."*

—Richard Brady,
founder Mindfulness in Education Network (MiEN)

"The quest for greater maturity and mindfulness in our educational system has an inspired expert guide in Amy Edelstein. Her important new book, The Conscious Classroom, *shows how deep wisdom can make a difference in the lives of at-risk youth. With an enjoyable mix of practical methodology, storytelling, and big picture thinking, it brings exciting new perspectives to the conversation about youth development. Students today are encountering a world of extraordinary complexity and they need educators and elders who understand that education is not only about knowledge—it's about learning and growing, self-knowledge and self-discovery, new insights and bigger contexts. Edelstein's Inner Strength System is a powerful ally in efforts to bring inner resilience, psychological empowerment, and cultural awareness to our nation's schools. May her work with young people flourish and may this important book bring hope and health to the next generation!"*

—Carter Phipps,
Senior Fellow, Institute For Cultural Evolution,
author of *Evolutionaries*

"This book is a wellspring of life-giving water in the heart of the contemporary educational desert. So simple: by inviting students to lay down the burden of over-thinking and the false imperative of over-consuming, we invite them into a vast field of stillness that reveals our essential interconnectedness, inspiring conscious action rooted in kindness for themselves and all beings. Amy Edelstein's clear and evocative

writing and thoughtful pedagogy conveys exactly how to facilitate this vital revolution."

—Mirabai Starr,
author of *Caravan of No Despair: A Memoir of Loss and Transformation* and *God of Love: A Guide to the Heart of Judaism, Christianity and Islam*

"In Philadelphia, the poorest large city in the nation, many children face multiple barriers to fulfilling their human potential. For every child that rises above the odds, imagine how many did not make it. These lifelong skills are a must for any young person who aims to fulfill their human potential and do more than simply survive. That is why the work of Amy Edelstein as detailed in The Conscious Classroom *is so critical. The Inner Strength System equips young people with the tools that breed resilience and emotional self-sufficiency. With these tools, they can stay grounded and rise above the tumult of an uncertain world."*

—Sharmain Matlock-Turner,
CEO Urban Affairs Coalition,
Senior Fellow Univ. of Pennsylvania
Fels Institute of Government

"Mindfulness is a path of practice that can help students, teachers, school leaders, and the entire school community live and learn better. By cultivating our inner capacity for greater awareness, we co-create flourishing school environments, offering students and especially teens practices toward greater understanding, compassion, and peace. Amy Edelstein's The Conscious Classroom *is a clear and strong voice to empower teens through mindfulness practices to navigate change, complexity, and culture."*

—Valerie Brown, J.D.,
Co-Author, *The Mindful School Leader: Practices to Transform Your Leadership and School*

The Conscious Classroom

The Inner Strength System™
for transforming the teenage mind

Amy Edelstein

For information contact Emergence Education Press, PO Box 63767, Philadelphia, PA 19147.

ISBN-10: 0-9995658-0-X
ISBN-13: 978-0-9995658-0-3

Library of Congress Control Number: 2017913582

Published in the United States of America by:

Emergence Education Press
P.O. Box 63767
Philadelphia, PA 19147

www.EmergenceEducation.com

For more on the Inner Strength System™ and Amy Edelstein's work:
www.InnerStrengthFoundation.net
and www.amyedelstein.com

Printed & bound in the United States of America

For all the children,
May you embrace the world with curiosity and hope.
May your educators embrace you with interest and Love.

For the students from Bodine High School, Class of 2016, the first Inner Strength teen mindfulness program:
You are in my heart.
I can't wait to see all that you will do.

Contents

FOREWORD | Thy Self, Thy World 1

PREFACE | Schools Today & the Markers of Our Time . . . 3

CHAPTER I | The Conscious Classroom 9
Recognizing the Lens We Use 14
Our World of Constant Change. 17
Becoming Aware 22
Educating for Emergence 23

CHAPTER II | Mindful Contemplation 25
The Art & Science of Reflection 33
Inner Strength for Outer Stability 35

CHAPTER III | New Vantage Points 39
Vistas for Connecting & Reflecting. 45
Untangling Negative Influences. 47
Love & Kindness in the Classroom 52
The Power of Cultural Context 55
Navigating Even Bigger Factors 59

CHAPTER IV | An Uncertain Age 61
Personal Experience & Global Shadows. 69
Working with Historical Levers. 82
The Plight & Prospect of Urban Schools 83

CHAPTER V | Change Agents in Our Midst 89
Sparking Curiosity 96
Trauma-Informed Mindfulness: A Humble Approach 100
Tools for Teen Anxiety & Depression 107
Fishing Skills for the Twenty-First Century 109

CHAPTER VI | The Quality of Our Relatedness 115
Is the Past Also the Present? 124
What Is a Paradigm Shift 127

CHAPTER VII | Looking Out from the Center 131
School Climate | Group Consciousness 138
Are We Solid or Flow? Wave or Sea? 145

CHAPTER VIII | Culture & Us 153
Footprints across Time 161
Girls, Boys & Our Embeddedness in Culture 167
Teens as Culture Changers 174

CHAPTER IX | Our Culture of Individuality 177
Free to Be Me, Questioning Our Self-Identity 182
Making Meaning 191

CHAPTER X | An Optimistic Future 197
Educating for a Better Future 204

Endnotes 207

About The Author 237

Contact 239

FOREWORD

Thy Self, Thy World

Contemplative practices, such as those taught by Amy Edelstein, are known to improve students' ability to relax, concentrate, regulate their emotions, and do better in school. While these important benefits pertain to the welfare of the individual student, the potential benefits of these practices to the school culture, to the community the student is a part of, and to society and culture at large have hardly been explored so far. Actually, one of the objections to incorporating such practices into the school curriculum is that they may make students *more* self-centered and self-absorbed. Even where the attitude toward "contemplative pedagogies" (inclusion of different meditative, contemplative, and dialogic practices in teacher training and the education field) has been very positive, such as recently in my country, Israel, the effects of these pedagogies *beyond* the individual have often been questioned—so far, without a clear answer. Indeed, what are or what could be those effects?

One of the main contributions of Edelstein's work lies in addressing this crucial question. Based on her own practice and experience, Edelstein is guiding her students to "connect the dots" between knowing and cultivating themselves, being caring and involved members of their community, and ultimately being active participants in an evolving world. In this book, as in her work, she eloquently does that by contextualizing contemplative practices within the precept "Know thyself" (considered the most important moral principle and philosophical practice in ancient philosophy) and contextualizing *this* adage within bettering the world (*tikkun olam*, in Hebrew).

The famous philosopher of education Jean-Jacques Rousseau started his article "On the Inequality among Mankind" with these words: "Of all human sciences, the most useful and most imperfect appears to me to be that of mankind: and I will venture to say, the single inscription on the Temple of Delphi [Know Thyself] contained a precept more difficult and more important than is to be found in all the huge volumes that moralists have ever written." Ultimately, it is the "science of mankind" which Edelstein is teaching her students, and reading her book one cannot but recognize that self-knowledge is not only an essential basis for self-cultivation, but is also the foundation of knowing, feeling, and caring for all of humankind, for the world, and beyond.

Amir Freimann
Founder, Israeli Education Spirit Movement

PREFACE

Schools Today & the Markers of Our Time

I walked past the LGBTQ[1] meeting posters in the entry hall and carried on into the principal's office. It was close to the end of the school year; graduation artifacts were sprouting on the walls; and the confidence as well as the decibel level of the students was rising.

It was a happy time. The year had gone well.

As my meeting with the faculty began, we talked about the principal's vision of a sanctuary room. A room for observant Muslim students to do their obligatory lunchtime prayers; a room for sensitive and confidential meetings between parents, students, and teachers; and most especially relevant to me, a room where students could lead mindfulness practices for other students during lunch and free periods.

"I would be happy to share my own practice with the students if that would help," the principal offered, "or tell them how much it helped my husband when his daughter died."

There was a tautness in the air, an unexplained tension. The other teacher and counselor at the table seemed strained. Usually there was laughter and affinity among these three. But not today.

"We'd need an adult in the sanctuary room if there are students in there," the counselor snapped. "We can't just put a couch in there with unsupervised teenagers." In spite of the tension, the image made me smile.

"And we can't ask teachers to give up more of their own time unless there is some type of compensation," threw in the English teacher, the school's union representative. On top of the fact that teachers haven't had a contract, secure pay, or any kind of increase in base salary or benefits for four straight years, it's a sore point to, in any way, imply that more might be asked of them. In Pennsylvania, it is actually illegal for teachers to strike. And so the situation remains painfully unresolved.

But that wasn't what was imparting a sense of edge.

This public school of five hundred students feels a lot like a family, and in families, there are often unspoken issues or issues not yet ready to be made public.

In schools these days you never know. Is it a union issue? A school board budget issue? A teachers' issue? An interpersonal issue? Before I walked into my next class with the kids, I learned what was behind the tension.

Over the past couple weeks not one, but three students had expressed suicidal thoughts and actions.

One, a bright and dedicated student, was now going to be hospitalized for a month. The others were in various states of shock and disassociation, not at all themselves. Their classmates didn't know yet, but they would soon. Supporting the rest of the students so new issues didn't balloon out of control preoccupied the faculty. Attending to these specific students, the loss of school time, the college prep tests missed that couldn't be made up…the repercussions were just beginning to ripple out. Yet the time available to nurture the kids and the number of staff on hand to respond to it all didn't change.

I didn't know what to say when the counselor told me. One of these students, a quiet, engaged, and composed teen was in one of my classes. She was gentle, smart, disciplined, engaged, interested in mindfulness, intent on being a psychologist. I had no idea so much sorrow lurked beneath the surface. She carried a family sadness from her earliest years. Circumstances beyond anyone's control brought those hardships to the forefront again, and she was caught in the middle. It was overwhelming and profoundly confusing for her. She wrote a letter from her state of overwhelm and was now swept up in a whirl of supervision, testing, and medication. The questions flew across my mind. Could I have seen more? Done more? Prepared her better to experience and manage what seems utterly disheartening and overwhelming?

One of the other students who was so deeply sad was frightened by his emerging sexuality. With so much social emphasis on gender identity, teens are pushed to declare their sexual preference. The new peer pressure is on "coming out." Without understanding the strains and consequences, teens feel compelled to declare their private intimacies before they are ready, before they are secure enough in their own choices and identity to make public something that is so private. Often, the pressure is to declare something that has not yet fully formed in their own consciousness. Too many times, students feel forced to confront these issues with their parents before they are equipped to deal with a parent's censure, anger, or rejection.

It was unclear what pushed the third student to vocalize his own sense of futility. In this case, it was not academics, not the enormous emphasis on standardized-test results, or college acceptance. It was also not brought on by bullying, peer pressure, or other school-related incidents. As far as the faculty knew, it was also something beyond the school's purview and control. Yet, whether a school is privy to the triggers or not, whatever happens in a student's life colors their ability to learn or even attend classes. And that becomes the school's responsibility. The world is confusing, and good guidance these days in many children's lives is limited. Understaffed schools, by default, pick up the pieces. They shepherd the students as best as they can.

With that end to a meeting I thought was going to be simply a planning session for the number of mindfulness classes the school would receive in the upcoming year, I walked into the classroom to lead the last lesson of the term on mindfulness and cultural development. My thoughts and feelings were swirling as I sat in my seat and looked out at the sea of open and trusting young faces. They didn't know yet. How will they feel when they did? I took up the mindfulness bell and began our introduction to make space for what is, to slip behind thought and feeling and discover a reservoir of strength and resilience. My own practice that day was filled with the roiling eddies and currents of the maelstrom of contemporary adolescent life.

Days like those have given me pause to think more deeply, and then think again. We don't have the luxury of time or resources to resolve all the factors leading to the impossible predicaments facing many of our schools and hundreds of thousands of our youth. Even with all the time and resources in the world, I don't think the way forward is yet clear. In many respects, it will be this generation of youth who need to find that loose thread to pull and unravel the skein of the world's issues. It will be on their watch that significant leaps are made to move us into a very different, and far more compassionate, harmonious, and wholesome future. So we must prepare them well.

In this book, I will lay out how seeing in context can make all the difference for all of us, especially for teens who are navigating their own inner challenges, and the bump-off effect for adults close to them who are also struggling. The Inner Strength System rests on being able to see events and experiences in context, which means learning to interpret our experience in light of the events surrounding it. Some of the tools that make this possible are the tools of mindful contemplation, as well as an appreciation for the long-term developmental history of the world, ourselves, and our culture. I hope to give you a better understanding of how mindfulness, developmental neurobiology, and the evolution of culture can powerfully transform a student's experience from one of overwhelm, anxiety, and victimization to one of interest, passion, and engagement.

As your own paradigm begins to shift and you start to feel into this emergent way of seeing, new options will appear to you as well. I hope (and intend to help) you develop faith, as I have, in the possibility of a wholesome and reasonable way forward for ourselves and our culture, a learning system that empowers the best of students and motivates them to reach for their higher human capacities and their deeper connections with themselves and one another. For in that ability to connect—with self, others, the world, cosmos, past, future—we create node points that spark with the current of possibility. In that connection and connectedness, we create channels for the juice of creativity to flow. Like a distributed electrical circuit board, our ideas will take new routes, join and rejoin others, and light up solutions.

As you learn to see the world in a larger context, you may find yourself pondering new options and insights. You will start to intuit answers to questions that seemed insurmountable from the vantage point you were looking from before. Questions like: How do we prepare students and create conscious classrooms to rise above challenges that are so varied, complex, and uncontrollable? How do we reframe what we see and access a reservoir of inner strength that promotes outer stability? How can we retrain our view of the world and create space and room to breathe? Seeing these questions and problems as inseparable from the flow of the past and the up-swell of the future, you'll realize that, given the reality of our short lives, you are in fact relieved of the full burden of answering all these questions on your own. You'll start to see how the next generation not only must, but also will, take up the reins of the future. With this type of preparation, our students today will become reliable stewards of what is to come. With the relief and integration of context, with the connectedness that arises from a process-oriented perspective, and with the heart that comes from a felt sense of our effect on everything around us, this generation of youth will, in their own unique and diverse ways, come up with pathways forward we never could have imagined. And that is where great hope lies.

Thank you for taking this journey with me. And thank you even more for opening to new ways of seeing in order to better mentor and better love our kids.

Amy Edelstein
Philadelphia, Pennsylvania
Fall, 2017

CHAPTER I

The Conscious Classroom

I watch the ripples change their size
But never leave the stream
Of warm impermanence and
So the days float through my eyes
But the days still seem the same
And these children that you spit on
As they try to change their worlds
Are immune to your consultations
They're quite aware of what they're going through
Changes…

David Bowie
"Changes"

What is a "conscious classroom?" How can we as educators create an environment that supports our students, ourselves, and a creative learning in the face of so many pressures, so much uncertainty, and so many individualized needs? Given the issues, creating a conscious classroom has to depend not on a set of constants but on a perspective or outlook that can take in, integrate, and create a meaningful hierarchy of importance among facts and events—and rejuvenate the self all at once. It's a tall order.

But it is, in fact, quite possible, without expensive tools, years of re-training, or unrealistic changes in contemporary school structures and protocols. If we would have to wait for those factors, we might as well put off significant change in the way we support our kids for the foreseeable future. As educators, parents, and adults who are concerned about the prognosis for our future, we can't afford to wait and leave this generation of kids unsupported now and unprepared to be stewards of our shared future. The Inner Strength System is both a set of practical, applicable classroom tools and, more importantly, a set of perspectives which significantly supports teens' resilience, well-being, and ability to manage challenging and complex issues. It simultaneously supports educators, for we all know that the degree of our own stress impacts our kids. The more resilient, flexible, and empowered we are, the better able we are to support our teens. And that can make all the difference.

So let's start at the beginning. What is happening in our age, and what is happening in the adolescent mind?

Kids in any era hit that stage where they realize everything is changing. Their bodies are changing, their self-sense is changing, their responsibilities are changing, their interests are changing, their access to the world is changing. And on and on it goes. Adolescence is almost synonymous with change. Some of those changes are long-standing, predictable, and welcome. And some, in the times we are living in, are fraught with systemic cultural shifts that turn adolescence into a precarious sea of choppy waves and uncertain tides.

Uncertainty is another word for change, for the fact that what we take to be solid is also in a state of flux. Quite literally, the ground beneath our feet or the chair we are sitting on is moving. If we look at the component parts of what we take to be solid at an atomic or subatomic level, we see particles in constant orbit. Our solidity is a world that is spinning—more space than substance. From that perspective, we are never the same moment by moment; the world is never the same moment by moment; we are always moving, and in motion. My father was a particle physicist, and he liked to challenge my siblings and me when we were young children to think about the atomic makeup of the table or door: "There's more space in this table at the atomic level than there is matter." I would press my small hand on the tabletop, trying to sense the electrons swirling around empty space in the wood. I would scrunch up my nose, wondering if the electrons were swirling around empty space in my fingers and trying to imagine where the empty space of my fingers ended and the empty space of the table began. Could I really locate a line where my hand and the table were entirely separate? Is everything, in the end when seen from that perspective, one continuous event? Was everything, even on a material level, really one, without separation? My own inquiry into this over the course of my professional life has led to as many questions as insights. *The Conscious Classroom* encourages the exploration of both answers *and* uncertainty as a model for our own development as educators and as a model for the way we teach students and prepare them for the future.

As futurist John Smart says, we live in a time where the rate of change is so fast that the world is approaching singularity (a vertical line climbing the x-axis of the graph of development). Learning to manage uncertainty is foundational if we, as educators, are going to prepare our teenagers for their future. Can the recognition of constant change, as a fact, flip life from frightening to soothing? Can the unceasing flow all around and within us become as comforting as the mist of a waterfall or the tides rolling in against the shore? There is an art and a perspective that allows us to turn our experience upside down. There is a vantage point that transmutes the fact of constant flux from an anxiety-producing experience to a reality that allows for enormous possibility.

A large part of education is helping youth become conscious and aware. To become conscious, we must become more aware and discriminating around how we are identifying and interpreting the significance of facts and events that occur all around us. We must identify the context that frames our experience and perhaps enlarge or change that scaffolding. Helping students see in context means teaching them how to understand and interpret vast sweeps of history that have brought us to this point as well as the fundamental natural patterns that shape our reality. Asking teenagers to reflect on the world they are in the midst of in the present tense is a tall order. And yet they can, and it has a profound effect.

As adolescents stretch to understand a broader and more inclusive perspective, something essential can shift for them. They discover that they *belong* at an existential level. They also learn to depersonalize their experiences, appreciating that there are so many large-scale forces at play that form us. We may be able to affect or influence these forces, but not entirely shift them. When students are able to see themselves as products of millions of years of biological formation and tens of thousands of years of cultural formation, the sheer scale is so large it becomes intriguing to them. Identifying these large-scale factors influencing their experience becomes fascinating rather than disempowering—a subject for curiosity, not overwhelm. By changing the vantage point and scope we bring into our view, without changing the facts, we can change our experience and our sense of inner strength. The value of seeing in context is not that it erases or removes obstacles or important conundrums. Rather, it empowers us with clarity, perspective, and inner stability to approach issues afresh. This leaves teens with a positive challenge and a future to lean into.

Recognizing the Lens We Use

Recognizing the framework we use to interpret reality is essential to being able to make sense and navigate the complex world. I advocate an approach where we "see in context," meaning we take in a variety of factors in the environment around us, in a historical timeline and in our own makeup, to help frame the facts and experiences we have. No matter how we view reality, consciously or more often unconsciously, we are seeing reality within the framework of a specific ideological context. Whether that context is Cartesian or monist, mythic or modern, cyclical or developmental, or informed by an entirely different philosophical framework, when we recognize that we are using a specific interpretive lens we are better able to question the usefulness of that lens. And when needed, update the prescription. Students are rarely taught that they see through a lens. Even more infrequently are they taught that there are multiple lenses which are all valuable that they can use to interpret the world around them, and the feelings within them.

Knowing that we see and interpret reality according to a specific context is especially valuable to students when they are confronting disturbing current events, inequities or unfairness, friction with parents, tension with what is perceived as "the system," or any of the multitude of issues adolescents find overwhelming, disempowering, or disturbing. This can be as simple as gaining some objectivity on intense emotions, or making the connection that cultural change affects our personal experience. When students learn just a little about making space and seeing their experience in a different framework, they become able to make sense of their world. They begin to express a sensitivity that belies their years.

At the end of the school year, I ask the students to describe what they've learned from engaging with mindfulness and seeing the world with more dimensionality, in context. They regularly give answers like this:

"I learned to look at things from multiple perspectives. When I am working on something tough, I can look at the benefits of whatever I'm working on to encourage myself to keep working on it. This way, something very boring or painful can become something fun."

"I learned about perspective with mindfulness. The teachers often talked about being in the present moment and separating yourself from your feelings, and this helped me see if I'm overreacting to things. For example, if this is bothering me right now, will it matter in a couple of days, weeks, or months or years?"

These straightforward expressions indicate an ability these teens gained to reflect on their experience. This skill is as empowering as it is flexible. This art of seeing in context enables students to dis-embed themselves from a troubling perspective. Being able to see a situation from a variety of viewpoints is an immediately practical, applicable, and empowering skill. Recognizing and shifting one's context or perspective is a little different than walking a mile in someone else's shoes. We are not simply changing perspectives; we are grokking that our unquestioned framework has its own embedded assumptions and preferences, its own prejudices and blindnesses.

Although classrooms are designed to impart *content*, in a conscious classroom seeing that *context* is as important as content changes the nature of conversations and provides powerful openings where there has been friction. One of the best ways we can prepare students to enter into positions of responsibility in a world that will look so different from the one we grew up in is to impart to them an ability to intuit and shift worldviews. Yet as important as it is, it is also no small task. Far too few of us have been trained to reflect on this aspect of reality ourselves, let alone teach this to our youth.

So as educators, we must begin to be able to objectify our biases, self-reflect on the potential distortions in our view. We all think we don't hold a specific worldview. We believe that our own worldview is simply how things are. But it's not so. As adults, we are able to self-reflect in this way, even if we are not accustomed to doing it. For teens, being able to objectify their worldview and learn how to see differently is a growth stage in and of itself. It requires guidance and emotional maturity. And it requires inner strength. Inner strength to allow the world to re-form and recalibrate along unanticipated lines. The more we believe we are directing the realignment, the more likely our new worldview will have feet of clay, weighted down to the swamp bottom of our familiar worldview. To travel freely, to embark on a quest that allows us to journey beyond the familiar, we must be willing to become quiet, porous to the tides of awareness that, like the breath, rolls in and then rolls out again. The Inner Strength System is a process that enables us to create the space and follow some practices to create a learning environment for this shift to occur.

Our World of Constant Change

For this moment, back to ch-ch-ch-changes....

Becoming conscious of change is an essential element of this approach. Flux and impermanence as qualities of the fabric of reality was something I was confronted with and challenged by throughout my education, starting from a very young age. The confrontation I experienced came most bluntly from the hard sciences. When we built models in science class of Styrofoam balls in orbit around larger Styrofoam balls representing oxygen or iron or carbon atoms, my young mind had a hard time understanding how the floor under our feet could be solid and in motion at the same time, and what did that mean about the constancy of the world we exist in and the anchors we hold on to? Or, when we used those same multi-sized Styrofoam balls to represent planets and moons in orbit around suns, the same conundrum confronted me on a macro scale. That massive object I stand on is not just changing on its surface or molten core; it is moving even as I stand here. Change, motion, flux, flow, process.[2] If I had come across the early twentieth-century mathematician and philosopher Alfred North Whitehead then, I might have been able to see that this motion is not to be feared, but rather seen as the expression of the creativity of all life, down to the smallest bit of matter and up to the greatest star. Process and that which "stands beyond, behind, and within the passing flux of immediate things"[3] are the profound contemplations he gave the last decades of his life at Harvard trying to understand.

From a process perspective, we see that this moment is not static. Understanding how this is so, paradoxically, creates security and stability. We no longer are trying to go against the world to find solid ground. We can then balance or flow with the changing seas. For students who are in the middle of the physiological and emotional turbulence of teenage years, finding a positive way to understand change can be profoundly helpful. During the adolescent years, so much within them and around them is changing, including how they perceive. Human developmental patterns, habits, and complex growth processes, which make us who we are, paint the arc of our lives from birth to death. Those changes are remarkable and also somewhat predictable. Opening the door to contemplate the interrelationship between these changes—e.g., how survival imperatives contribute to certain aspects of brain growth or how maturation of parts of the brain affect a teen's perception of risk—rather than simply trying to pin down variables like butterflies in a species collection helps teens see the beauty, wonder, and interrelationships of factors illustrating the way their lives, their selves, and the world unfolds.

In the Inner Strength System, students contemplate growth and capacity, seeing the development of potentials as well as the loss of outdated functionality, and learn that growth and little deaths are part of the fabric of the universe. We don't need to teach all the specifics that link causes to effects. It is enough to point to some of the wonders of biological, cultural, or social questions to get teens thinking about the world in this way. How does the brain form from just a single egg and sperm? How does that brain grow in conjunction with our nervous system and respiratory system? How does it learn to store memory and emotion? And for that matter, how did our eyes learn to "see"? What do teens experience now that they didn't as infants, toddlers, pre-teens? How is change part of the fabric of life? When teens become fascinated by the changing world around them, they become more comfortable with flux and flow, less afraid of the unknown future ahead, less desperate for a world of immutable constants. They become curious about the changes in their bodies, their perceptions, their bonding patterns, even their ability to contextualize or weigh consequences. They learn to become comfortable with the way things actually are.

Learning how to understand our experience and self in this context of process,[4] we realize that however good or bad our experience is, however much we like or dislike what is occurring around us, there will be movement and change. Can we become comfortable with the fact that we are standing on shifting sands, that the ground beneath our feet has more space than solidity? The longing for security, while deeply important for our well-being, growth, and ability to blossom into our higher potentials, can be met differently than how we traditionally expect it to be. Rooting the quality of our relatedness in our experience of the process-oriented nature of reality gives us stability to withstand all kinds of storms. This is not an attitude or perspective we can effectively "apply" in a specific instance, though that conscious application helps. This is a different order or way to understand reality, and once we awaken to this at a deep level, we will see reality differently. When we educate our youth with this orientation to the world around them, their personality structure becomes more flexible and resilient, more kind and more hopeful. It also releases a degree of existential strain. No longer pushing back against the nature of reality insisting that it be something that it is not—e.g., solid and permanent rather than in motion and changing—youth will work with the way things are rather than futilely endeavoring to control, manage, or resist the very way they are made up.[5]

A process orientation changes so much, from the esoteric to the practical. For the student who receives a lower test score than she wanted, this recognition can prevent a descent into sadness, self-hatred, or despair. Twenty percent[6] of teenagers these days suffer from depression, suicidal ideation, and even physical violence against themselves. From a worldview that takes into account large-scale factors of movement or change, a teen can look out from her disappointment onto a mapping of reality that shows each event as part of a larger flow with all kinds of possibilities emerging from any specific point. This understanding viscerally communicates that no single number is a final pronouncement on her identity or future. It also helps her see that how she responds to her grade now also has an effect on what she believes will be possible in the future. Then she can put into practice her mindfulness practices to accept things as they are, extend self-acceptance, and reach for a better outcome.

For the student whose father received harsh sentencing for a minor infraction and cannot raise the money for bail or appeal, it alleviates personal guilt in the midst of the pain. Seeing the larger picture and so many forces at play[7] provides the basis to recognize that all kinds of interconnected causes and effects are in motion.

It is neither his fault nor his father's fault that they are unable to combat the injustice quickly, or perhaps at all. For students who struggle under denial, despair, or the desire to cut off, this appreciation for large causes in motion, for macro influences, can reduce personal guilt. Personal guilt over something we have no control over is profoundly disempowering. For too many inner-city teens from poverty, that is one experience that needs to be reinterpreted in a more accurate and useful context.

The visceral experience of process can also bring a modicum of hope that unexpected events may open new, previously unseen possibilities. Circumstances may shift in unexpected ways. Unanticipated human connections and resilience can emerge, as a father and son learn how to maintain a relationship under challenges and separation. A youth may find the moral courage to become a powerful and authentic voice for reform. As educators, the more we see the world through this lens and hold for these possibilities, the more we create space for new potentials to emerge. If we are drowned in a perspective that doesn't give us sufficient distance from challenging circumstances, we will not be able to serve our students (or ourselves) with an optimism and positivity that comes from inner space and a deep seeing into the nature of things.

Once we awaken to the pervasiveness of change and start to look at how life really works—that everything is in some sort of motion—we begin to see how deeply interconnected everything is. Recognizing the far-reaching way we are all affected by forces so much beyond our control changes our sense of being in the world. The far-reaching implications of this sort of flux are also referred to as *interdependence*, *cause and effect*, or *influence*. Rather than seeing ourselves as merely isolated, independent, or static individuals, we recognize that we are part and parcel of the flow and process of life unfolding. Factors and forces larger than our individual actions and will connect us one to another to such a degree that we can no longer see ourselves as isolated parts. We are profoundly linked and interconnected. When it begins to dawn on teens how interconnected they are, something significant changes. They recognize they are no longer alone or separate. They become able to depersonalize their experience of insecurity in the face of overwhelming changes. In a classroom it equalizes things. It puts everyone on the same team, together. It connects cliques; it links the social with the shy. Every teen, like each of their classmates, is being formed by great forces that are always in motion. Insecurity is not a personal issue to solve; it is an understanding about the nature of things to be applied.

Becoming Aware

Mindfulness and other contemplative practices help us be still enough to reflect on the significance of these more foundational qualities of the world around and within us. They allow us to become conscious of more subtle aspects of our experience. Mindfulness allows us to become conscious and explore the qualities of human consciousness in our own experience. Contemplative practices teach us to be with what is. They help us make space so we can begin to reflect on our own beliefs, which are as close to us as our own skin. They cultivate in us the ability to be still and at rest, to be with joyous insights or painful facts. They allow us to be at peace with loss and grief and to weather the reverberations of fear, anxiety, and trauma. To grow, we must start from where we actually are. We must first see and be with who we are as we are. Then we can lean into new paradigms and new possibilities. I will speak more about the specific mindfulness approach I recommend in the sections to come.

Educating for Emergence

Emergent education is a way of training that puts great stock in and draws on teens' creativity and their love for something new. In my approach to stimulate this type of curiosity, I teach kids how to rest in themselves and cultivate a familiarity with their own capacity to be aware. From that expansive ground, as we've discussed, they view the world from a perspective of constant change; they understand the implications of cause and effect, and they develop a sensitivity to the profound interconnectivity of all things. Teens learn to interpret reality and their own life experience from a perspective that has the greatest chance of revealing unexpected insights, generating punctuated emergence, and sparking discontinuous discoveries. Furthermore, learning to see the context or framework in which they are setting their experience gives students the understanding that *how* we frame our experience is as important as *what* the experience is. Teaching systems-thinking enables students to hypothesize specific solutions to individual issues while appreciating the integral nature of all factors involved, the sense of a whole as greater than or distinct from just its parts. *Merriam-Webster* defines *emergent* as that which arises unexpectedly, that is newly formed, or that which arises as a natural consequence. In a conscious classroom, where our goal is education for whole child wellness and a creative future, fostering the conditions for emergence create the best possibilities for unexpectedly positive outcomes for each individual child and for the collective learning experience of the classroom as a whole.

CHAPTER II

Mindful Contemplation

I am who I am
That is that
I am who you are looking back
You are who I am
Can you imagine that?

Joy to the world
Peace on the earth
God bless the children
How we love them.

Guru Singh, Seal & friends
"I Am"

Creating Space

Let's step back for a minute and spread before us the pieces that make up a teen's experience right now. Self-image, aspiration, romance, physical prowess, academic pursuit, friendship, social status, fashion, creative voice—to name a few of the aspects of self-identity that are at play. Lay them on the table of your mind, like a diviner's mesa, without trying to make sense of all the pieces first. Our ability to educate, more than just to impart information, rests on our ability to be comfortable with not already knowing, with resting in front of an array of puzzle pieces without being clear what picture they will make. Are you able to do that? Can you do that in your own life? Can you do that in the midst of a tense moment with a recalcitrant student? Can you hold space? Be honest. Most of us don't recognize, or won't admit, our own challenges with complexity or uncertainty. Too many in positions of authority prefer to act decisively and protect themselves against uncertainty rather than hold space and see what emerges.

Educating to help students seek for and recognize new or emergent possibilities means we bias that uncertainty. We come to see it as the best ground to move from. It aligns us with the fact that we simply don't know all the pieces and the answers. Aligning with the facts of process and complexity, being attune to the profundity of cause and effect, we put ourselves in the best position to allow a new response to emerge from us. If our intention is to support, nurture, inspire, illuminate, and awaken, new possibilities will become apparent to us. Opening wide to let in as much of the picture as possible at first seems like it could drown us, but, in fact, it provides a sense of safety.

The first steps of this process are opening up wide and seeing everything as it is. Meditation is one of the best-practiced methods, but there are many pathways. When I refer to meditation, I use that term also as a placeholder for a variety of contemplative practices and styles. This first step involves learning how to embrace more of reality in our awareness. We need to see the important pieces and their relationship to the whole, to see the background and how it holds everything in context. Then we have to apply ourselves and connect the dots.

Try it for a few minutes:

Sit still, and allow the world to be as it is. Each time your thoughts or memories get overwhelming, each time you want to push something out or avoid what is coming into your awareness, take a deep breath and without trying to fix or manipulate it, just let it be as it is. Let it all be.

Imagine you are lying on your back on a warm summer's night under the night sky, gazing at the stars. Notice the innumerable dots of light, the planets and distant suns, the moving meteors and satellites and planes. Shift your attention ever so slightly from the pinpricks of light to the space between them. Let yourself follow the blackness of the night sky as far as it goes in any direction. Notice how the sky doesn't seem to be bothered by any of the objects floating in it. Let your attention rest on that backdrop of space. Let your attention rest on the backdrop of consciousness rather than on the objects, the thoughts, feelings, sounds, that arise in your mind's eye. Every time you notice your attention back on the objects that arise in the field of consciousness, shift them back to the space, the infinite field they arise within.

Notice the sense of space.

Allow yourself to rest.

Without needing to change anything, let the stars be, rest in the sky, vast and easy, and unperturbed by whatever it seems to contain.

When the privileged prince Siddhartha Gautama sat under a tree, he determined to do just that. He proclaimed that he was not going to move toward temptation or away from threat until he was able to let things be as they are, to see things clearly. For strength, he stretched the fingers of his right hand, made his pledge to himself, and touched the ground, saying, "As the earth is my witness." When that determined nobleman stood up at the dawn, his insight led him to be known as the one who awoke from confusion. Of course, we know him as the Buddha. You can still sit under a descendent of this very tree, twenty-five hundred years later, touch the same ground with your own fingers, and determine to be still, let things be, and allow understanding to arise from there.

I sat and practiced all night one night in 1985 in the dusty town of Bodh Gaya, northern India. That gesture and what it represented kept me going through the night as I strove to be with what is, quiet my own mind, and bear all its shadows, fears, and inner demons. An enormously simple gesture like this confronts us with our acute fears and intense desires. Our own passion for unobscured clarity and our longing for a new way forward will get us through. Our conviction in our higher capacities for harmony and purpose help us see through the changing fluctuations of intense feelings and fears. The classroom can be a cauldron, cooking up intense feelings. Ultimately, as conscious teachers and role models, our ability to be steady in the midst of our own inner storms transmits ease and strength to our students. The calm that comes from our inner wrestling matches and victories helps our students develop confidence. It encourages them to find their own way, chart their own course, make decisions, and take actions that only they can see. We communicate the possibilities, teach them the skills, and create space for them to discover.

When I tell my students about the experience that made me most appreciate the power of meditation, I always wonder if the drama of it is too much. But my victory over adversity earns their respect. I show them what's possible. And that matters.

Here's what happened. After more than thirty years of sustained and often intensive contemplative practice, the moment that changed my conviction in the value of these tools, perhaps more than any of the epiphanies I'd experienced up until then, was one that is not uncommon and one I wouldn't wish on anyone else.

> *Over half a dozen years ago I was returning to my home in rural western Massachusetts. I'd been working in Manhattan and had returned partway by train. The last forty-five-minute leg was a beautiful drive through the bucolic countryside. The roads winding, the fields lush with early corn, the sunlight sending sparkling beams through gaps in the trees. It began to rain, that soft gray, light summer rain, and then day began to turn to dusk.*
>
> *The next thing I knew, I felt this strange sensation of being caged, crushed, unable to move. There were searing sensations coursing through my hips, a crunchy wetness in my mouth and on my face. My legs and feet were an odd blank that screamed with intensity. I opened my eyes to see a shat-*

tered side window, the steering wheel pinned to my chest, with no memory of how I got there. Neuroscientists say that the brain secretes a memory-erasing chemical to protect us from events our systems can't process, and I understand why. It was a head-on collision with an eighteen-wheel tractor trailer hurtling thirty-five miles an hour towards me. Fortunately, I had slowed to a crawl thanks to speed traps just up the road. Years ago the local police chief had lost his own child on this road, and he did not want anyone to lose another.

My consciousness began to roll in and out. Panic, pain, lucidity, confusion. I couldn't inventory the parts of me. Was that sensation phantom or real? Raw fear washed over me in waves like a riptide that wanted to pull me into it. Before long, out of nowhere some thirty people appeared, circling as if in a slow dance. They pointed and shouted, then moved to wrest some corner of the twisted metal open and extricate my frame. Each time they pulled, a scream roiled up from within me.

"Honey," a firefighter barked, the heavy metal-cutting Jaws of Life in his hand, "you're going to have to be quiet if we're going to get you out."

All of a sudden, I was aware of everyone around me in stark relief. Aware of their focus and attention, their concern and care. I was aware of a field of interconnectedness between us. Of a sense of space and of the current of vitality that seems to be part of the essence of our human consciousness. I was aware of a way to let go and be present without panic. And I was simultaneously aware of the abyss of fragmentation and fear overwhelming my psyche.

My years of contemplative practice had etched grooves of familiarity with this inner space into my experience. Without thinking, I could feel that sense of presence and stillness. I could feel how connected we all were. Not just esoterically, but quite directly, everyone was connected to me through their focus and attention, and we were all connected in a field of awareness. It flashed on me that it would be selfish not to keep my attention together with everyone else. Any insight, direction or unexpected clue that could possibly save my life might depend on my willingness to stay present. Their efforts could be obscured if I let myself fall into the abyss of physical and mental terror.

This moment counted. No one knew what the future would hold. If these were to be my last moments of clarity or of consciousness at all, I wanted them to be an expression of the best of what I'd learned. I wanted all my years of practice to count. I wanted my life to be an expression of my higher ideals. And so I moved away from the cliff of pain and fear and stayed present and connected. From that moment on, I never felt victimized or overwhelmed. Without effort or intensity I was able to stay steady in that moment and through all that was yet to come.

That's when I knew the power of this type of mindful awareness, of the reservoir of inner strength we can cultivate, and how important it is that we do so. We can create a familiarity with a space that contains even the most challenging events, a place we can rest in when we least expect to, but when we truly need to. This power of perspective and awareness is what I teach students now, and they respond to it amazingly well.

The Art & Science of Reflection

You can see the power of mindful awareness and the stability it can bring. There are many resources to learn these practices and technological tools from a growing number of insightful teachers, and my own guidance is available in other books. In this section I want to very briefly lay out the fundamentals of how to begin to make space in your own experience. I have included more detailed instructions and access to audios in the endnotes.[8] The space for mindful contemplation provides us with the wherewithal to be with what is deeply challenging, to step back from our unquestioned assumptions and beliefs, and also to see in a way that develops confidence in our own perception and experience without the rigidity of fixed and limiting conclusions.

Basic mindfulness practices have us rest our attention on a simple, universal object—a pleasing sound like a bell, the rise and fall of our breath, the sensation of our feet touching the floor. As we rest our attention on one of these elements, it allows us to sink into ourselves and leave the cacophony of thought and feeling on the surface of our awareness. Thought, feeling, memory, and emotion don't have to disappear. We simply leave them alone, using breath, sound, and sensation as anchors to hold our attention. With practice, mindful awareness lets us see what is happening within, without getting entangled with it. If you've ever tried to watch your breath or focus on the quality of being aware (rather than the objects that we are aware of), you'll know that the first thing that happens is all the things creating static in your brain come to the forefront. Your to-do list. Something you forgot. Something you said that you wish you hadn't. And on and on. "Oops, I was supposed to be watching the air going in and the air going out. Back to the breath." It seems so simple. And it is. This time-honored approach has been helping people gain clarity, perspective, and control for a couple of millennia. It is also easy to implement in a classroom. Kids can practice anywhere, at their desks, on the bus, in their beds, no props needed.

Paying attention to the inhalation and exhalation generally has a soothing and quieting effect. It allows for integration between the input centers of our system. The body has three neurological centers: around the gut, the heart, and of course the brain. Students can also watch their breath with one hand on their chest and one resting on their abdomen, gently following the rise and fall. When teens settle and synchronize these three information centers, they feel less pulled in different directions, more able to know who they are and what they feel, more integrated. This gives them strength to create a reliable hierarchy of their feelings and intuitions in the moment, to think independently, and to create a stable core so they can connect with others without fear of losing themselves.

In the classrooms I work with, students learn seven evidence-based tools. We work with mindful breathing, mindful body, open awareness, thought bubbles, love and kindness, attention to sound, and seeing things freshly or mindful eating. These practices are simple to learn and can have powerful effects. In different ways, they each help students learn how to be present, grounded, curious, connected to their physicality, and able to see the mundane with fresh eyes. Each of the practices can be modified and worked with creatively. They each lead to a variety of discoveries and give students different pathways to calm, focus, and relax.

Students recount that the act of paying attention to all five senses while they eat, explore, or see the relationship between desire and the body's response helps them work with a variety of eating disorders and change their eating habits to make more healthy choices. They work with body awareness, consciously relaxing muscles from head to feet. Many students work with the body scan to alleviate insomnia or to orient themselves before a big sports event. With the love and kindness contemplations students send caring wishes for well-being and peace to someone they love, to themselves, to kids they are having issues with, to strangers, and to the whole class, school, or neighborhood. Students describe over and over how they feel happier and feel care for others in a way they hadn't previously felt they needed to. Many describe relief from being able to dial back anger and vengefulness in tangible ways.

Contemplations like these can be taught in almost any classroom with simple instructions. Mainly, students need to feel free to experiment and become scientists of themselves, watching, observing, and repeating those contemplative activities over time to see what kind of changes they can make. Time and again, in privileged and underprivileged classrooms, kids movingly share their delight at the discoveries and changes they've made as they learn to become facile with mindfulness techniques.

Inner Strength for Outer Stability

The mindful awareness I teach emphasizes making space for our experience while not getting lost or overwhelmed by it. It encourages us to feel into what our physicality is like, the sensations in our bodies, the pull of gravity, the upward stretching of our spine. Some exercises point our attention to the backdrop of awareness in which the objects of our experience arise. Learning to make space, like the exercise of looking at the night sky instead of paying attention to the stars, planets, and meteors that cross it, we learn to pay attention to the backdrop of awareness itself, not the objects—the thoughts, feelings, physical sensations—that cross our mind's eye. This emphasis on creating space enables us to be with our experience, without being overwhelmed by it.

As a little mind experiment, take your hand and cover your eyes. What do you see? When you press your hand right up against your eyes (try it so you get the visceral experience), all we see is darkness or the vague lines of our fingers or palms. This is what it's like when a worry, problem, or fear is right on top of us. We are so close to it, so identified with it, that is all we see.

Now move your palm out just an inch or two. Now what do you see? A little light, a little more definition of your hand, a little more detail, a hint of a world beyond it. When we get just a little bit of space or objectivity on our experience, we can see the issue or problem more clearly, with more detail, better understanding.

Now stretch your hand as far from your face as it goes. Now what do you see? You see the whole room, which provides context. Maybe you are at home, at work, in a coffee shop or a park. That environment has resources, and you arrived there by specific means, using a variety of skills and strengths. Are there other people in that room, in your life? When we see with more space, we notice resources in ourselves, in our relationships, in the society around us. We see that we are not on our own. We see alternative routes around the object (thought, feeling, problem) that had been overwhelming and connect with new ways to respond, solve, or be with it. That's the power of being able to make space.

Grounding our experience in the immediacy of the present through the anchor of the breath or the sensations in our bodies allows us to arrive in our lives. Too many of us feel like walk-ins in our own bodies. We go through experiences without feeling like we were really there. We feel boredom and don't know how to alleviate it. Television, video games, or alcohol temporarily relieve that boredom, but we are again left with ourselves; often a dull sense of dis-ease or feeling lost takes hold again. Becoming more connected with the sensations in our bodies teaches us to see things freshly, to be present. That sense of connecting with our physicality cultivates a type of curiosity in the life process, in what it feels like to be alive. When we train ourselves to notice things as we're walking, how does the sun feel on our face? What do the trees look like swaying in the wind? What are the textures of the stone buildings around us? Becoming aware of natural textures, light, or movement has the effect of landing us in our lives.

CHAPTER III

New Vantage Points

I can see clearly now, the rain is gone,
I can see all obstacles in my way
Gone are the dark clouds that had me blind
It's gonna be a bright, bright
Sunshiny day.

I think I can make it now, the pain is gone
All of the bad feelings have disappeared
Here is the rainbow I've been prayin' for
It's gonna be a bright, bright
Sunshiny day.

Johnny Nash
"I Can See Clearly Now"

Higher Vantage Points

It is hard to truly get our heads around the way reality looks in different contexts. When we rise to a higher vantage point or embrace a broader perspective, we do see more. The intellectual art of being a generalist, of being able to take in, assimilate, and make sense of the big picture requires us to be comfortable holding this kind of a broad perspective. It requires us to get over our fear of heights. In a relentless twenty-four-hour news cycle that is increasingly being defined by 140 characters or instant photo uploads from halfway around the world, being able to see the big picture helps us look down at the blizzard of activity and discern meaning. And from meaning we can derive our way forward.

How many times have I walked into a schoolroom to find myself in the midst of a gripe session that doesn't really release any steam? I'm sure you know the kind of talk that goes around and around, kicking up dust, but no solutions arise, and no one seems able to lift their head up and out of the sandstorm to say something that lets everyone move on. Educators need to learn how to expand the context, which will change the way a problem is being approached. It will help us all make our precious discussion time more fruitful, constructive, and enriching. Teachers who have internalized this way of working with context communicate trustworthiness and openness. They become ballasts for teens. In a world that often seems unsettling and frightening to youth, the mere presence of a grounded, reliable, and flexible adult can make all the difference.

This way of working with issues is as much art as science, as much perseverance as it is surety. If you've ever walked a long way up a high mountain, you know the path you traverse looks much easier from above than it did when you were ascending, step by step. But simply telling yourself that does not make it so. You have to walk, one step at a time. Educators who train their students to view while being aware of the context they are using walk *with* their students. Significant shifts occur for students when, for the first time, they peer out at their position in the world from a vantage point that offers a greater vista. They see many more possibilities than they ever intuited were possible.

When I was in my early twenties, I spent twelve months walking on my own in various parts of the Himalayan mountain range. It was well before the era of cell phones, internet, and satellite maps. I would set off from a tiny village, find a little footpath up the mountain, and go. One stride after another on trade routes or herding paths, pilgrim paths or village supply roads would take me from adventure to adventure. I travelled alone so that I could connect with locals wherever I was, walk with them, visit with them, experience a life so far from the one I grew up in. Many days I walked alone long hours in the stillness, up one mountain face, switching back and forth and back and forth across the scree. The ascents were hard. Afraid of heights, I would regularly find myself holding my breath or talking my way across a narrow rope bridge hundreds of feet above a roaring steel-grey river. Once I came across two yogis seated on a glacial mouth, wrapped defiantly in light cotton shawls, practicing TUMO *(inner heat generation). The steam rose from their bodies and plumed over their heads. The sun was setting, and a cold shadow was creeping down the cascade of ice towards them. I was moved by their focus and somewhat frightened by their austerities. Leaving their practice undisturbed, I bounded by them, continuing up and up.*

There's nothing quite like the moment at the pinnacle's pass, jagged triangle tips of high peaks stretching below you, clouds snuggling into the valleys, and the view spreading for mile after unobscured mile. Higher than an airplane and with very little taller than you, the lap of the earth opens out far below, and life feels rarified and very far away. A quality of awareness and immediacy, of seeing, emerges when the stuff we usually see is so far below. Teeming villages and cities are hidden from view in the crevices and folds of the earth's great plates. From that vantage point, I felt like I could fly. No obstacles in my way, the groaning, creaking of aching feet and calves, the paralyzing vertigo that appears when you are peering thousands of feet down, the hunger and light-headedness from air so thin it feels like a gossamer veil. In that expanse, I felt the exaltation of the human heart and the open canvas of the future. In that space, emotional tangles from the past found room to unknot and dissolve. Impossible challenges were contextualized into something with greater breadth and depth. Space and compassion revealed themselves in the room to accept or grieve what cannot be changed and what had been lost. These moments changed me. Maybe not immediately. But subtly. And significantly. That's when I first began to understand the power of a higher vantage point to help unravel the knots of the heart and mind.

In the inner city where poverty, pollution, and privatization have led to so many fractures in our society, a unifying vantage point that invites is essential to give kids the courage to cross boundaries. This is more than metaphor. In our time, some Bronx kids grow up never taking the subway to the cultural center in the heart of Manhattan. Some South Philadelphia kids never see the greatest impressionist art collection in the world fifteen blocks away, even though its collector, Albert Barnes, wanted it to be available to Philadelphia's bricklayers, cooks, and street cleaners (not to art critics and the elite). And some Oakland kids have never crossed the bay to see the sun swallowed up by the Pacific Ocean at dusk. To create change, these kids need to be empowered with tools and a curiosity about life that is not superficial. Tools that generate insatiable fascination, that give boldness and stability, not from arrogance but from understanding and empathy, are the ones that can make a real difference. To shift the levers of prejudice and segregation, we need courage. A higher vantage point reveals reservoirs of strength we didn't know were there. Though we live in a time where kids can do amazing things, the simplest human connections can be elusive. The blinders that separate us from each other can be all but welded on. Though a student may be able to code an app on her phone or video-call a peer in a country 10,000 miles away, she still needs what feels like superhero strength to break down barriers in her own school. The power of accessing a reservoir of stillness and seeing all of the issues that sting contextualized in broad swaths of time gives kids the resources to hold grief and hardship. That ability builds confidence, strength, and love.

Vistas for Connecting & Reflecting

It is challenging to reflect on that which we find ourselves in the middle of. That is why it is hard for us to read the warnings of great sea changes in our environment even when those signs are all around us. And that is why a teen's quiet distress and the small alerts can be all but invisible to those he lives with.

Visionary thinkers have the ability to step up and peer out at the world and at others while remaining connected with that world and inseparable from the deeper currents of the vast unfolding process of life. They are able to be immersed in life *and* able to step up and out of it to see larger implications, trends, and possibilities. Great educators are visionaries. They make this broad perspective their vantage point. They are able to be present with the immediacy of what's happening in their classroom and see the meaningful implications, trends, and influences. They connect with one troubled student without losing the thirty-two other teens, each with their own issues. Teachers have to hold current events, issues with the school board, pressure from the teachers' union, questions from their colleagues, their personal circumstances all at once. Conscious educators embody a frame of reference that lets them recognize the influence those factors have on their own mood, their interpretation of events, and most especially, on their belief in what is possible. They can be with negative or destructive issues and still be rooted in a pervading optimism, buoyed by deeper values and higher aspirations. Our own optimism and objectivity rests on our ability to contextualize and to gain distance from troubling situations. It rests on our ability to draw from an inner source of strength, especially in those times that are more contentious.

What makes that kind of a stretch manageable? How do we as educators, parents, and mentors span the distance so we are both present and can see contextually? How do we reach through all those layers of our own awareness without fraying the delicate fabric of ourselves? As the high rates of burnout[9] in the helping professions attest, most of us don't do that well. We connect, but at a cost. We protect ourselves. Also at a cost. Far too many youth, as our teens describe, have an increased sense of alienation and are not able to feel the love that motivates most teachers. Yet that love is there. I see it in the many dedicated educators I come in contact with. They are every day heroes. The dedication they have to helping their students grow is a special sauce, one that enables them to endure the challenges of their profession day after day.

While releasing kids' potential may be the special sauce that keeps us going, we all need a way to replenish our stock. A conscious classroom relies on the constant renewal of optimism and the joy of learning. Renewal is not just a thing we do—it is a perspective or vantage point we see from. Mindful awareness alters our perspective and perception. It changes our vantage point. It helps us perceive subtlety. What we experience is more space. More room to maneuver in our own skin. This rejuvenates us from the inside out. The insights that come from being still, present, and at peace with ourselves provide a reservoir of strength.

As we learn to see this way, to be with what is, without grasping after a brass ring of static security, we discover a new orientation to our experience. Like polaroid glasses in the harsh sun, this view relaxes our eyes. It lets us perceive the details and contours of the classroom landscape that we miss when we are perpetually squinting, bracing ourselves against the onslaught of incoming issues. More relaxed in our stance, we can see ourselves, and our students, more clearly. We can better discern who they are, where they come from, and the direction they are heading without limiting where they might go.

Untangling Negative Influences

We do live in times when violence, separation, and fear have eroded our ability to educate in a way we would have loved to be educated. We live in a time when the gap between the wealthy and the majority of the population has created a highly stratified and dysfunctional education system. To rise above the debilitating pettiness of cultural and interpersonal bickering all too common these days, we probably find ourselves more often than not needing to take a deep breath. Instead of bracing ourselves against the incoming, there is a different skill to cultivate. That comes from being able to take in factors so large that we develop a very different understanding and much more compassion towards those issues that are irritating us at any given moment. What I'm advocating is more than just understanding a student's psychology, family, or trauma history, or socio-economic pressures. The Inner Strength System relies on taking large-scale influences or trends into account. This view gives us a sense of space and understanding that helps us connect with our students and with the wonder that inspired us to enter into a teaching role in the first place.

It is my belief, and my experience working with several thousand students in the inner city schools of Philadelphia, that by unpacking the philosophical insights of process or impermanence, unity and interconnection, and restful, nonjudgmental awareness students will be able to better order their world and their relationships. They'll be better able to learn and to care about what they are learning. When we educate our youth around these principles and teach them skills to rest in the vast space of the conscious mind, we can truly prepare them for an unknown future. We will also have a wonderful time creating authentic relationships with them along the way.

The philosophical and practical implications of this are significant and will change how we teach individuals and view the world around us. Right/left, black/white, bright/dull, we still inhabit the same environment. How we deal with issues and how we train students to deal with differences, frictions, and challenges changes when we recognize that solutions and course corrections must have a positive impact on the whole. Applying this is both specific and intuitive. What effect will the way we give out praise and discipline have on the whole over the long run? Being able to consider how an action will play out because of our appreciation for the underlying inseparability of all, for cause and effect, and for constant unfolding will inform our responses. It will also elicit more self-care and care for the whole, which we all certainly need. When these elements inform the scaffolding of our interpretative framework, our familiar self-sense is buttressed by something that seems paradoxical: flexibility.

We are so accustomed to viewing and analyzing discreet events, and to searching for solidity wherever we can find it, that the idea of seeking the insecurity of constant flux is an anathema to our system. We have a visceral allergic reaction, it seems, towards change. Changing jobs or houses and separating from a loved one are listed as some of the top stressors.[10] Why? The emotional and practical instability and flux creates dis-ease. Almost any teacher can tell you that managing the instability of transitions well can make all the difference in a classroom experience. As curious as human primates are, we crave stability. Viewing the world from a process-oriented perspective helps us make understandable that which makes us feel uncertain, and that creates stability.

One of the key methods for untangling the web of negative influences is not to only address them head-on. It is first to expand the framework in which we are seeing or experiencing them. As we've already seen, truly leaning into an integrated understanding of process is profound. The recognition that everything is part of an unfolding momentum and in a state of constant change creates personal stability. In Western philosophy this view is known as *process philosophy*. In Eastern schools of thought, it is known as *impermanence*. *Influence* can be understood as the momentum and long-term reverberation or impact of any action or event on everything else, the nature of cause-and-effect. The fundamental inseparability of all things, our essential interconnectedness or unity, is a corollary of the recognition of constant movement. When we begin to break down the world around and within us, we begin to see everything as brought into being, affected by, or influencing all else around us. This has a practical effect. It changes our perception of ourselves as alone or disconnected. Once we have looked deeply, whether we feel isolated or connected, we are still intrinsically connected to everything around us, breathing the same air, existing in the same universe.

We usually see things in terms of static objects. A process-oriented perspective looks at the movement or fluid relationship rather than static objects in proximity to one another. While this doesn't change *what* we are looking at, it changes *how* we understand the world. The fluidity of this perspective cultivates flexibility and resilience. Understanding the interconnected nature of all things is a perspective that informs us as educators, parents, mentors, or role models. Then we can connect the dots for kids. By linking a youth's experience with the reality of constant change, the long-term consequences of actions, and the profound interconnectedness of all things, we can help students line up their experience. Like the child's birthday game spider's web (where a child moves around a room with a ball of yarn, connecting points and untangling a room-sized web to get their prize), when children learn to connect the dots, they can feel into their own wonderful and overwhelming experience. They learn how to see the flow of their experiences not as frightening projectiles coming at them but as a single flow, one that is as varied and connected as the diamond drops of water that form a thundering waterfall.

Seeing in this developmental and holistic context is one of the most powerful tools to equip our youngsters and ourselves with. This skill and perspective serves us regardless of what arises in our experience, regardless of what occurs in the world around us, and regardless of what our kids aspire to become. It helps students grow into themselves at their own pace, open to new portals of discovery that are appearing on their own horizons. Its framework of unity and nonseparation allows kids to connect to others and to the world around them. The Inner Strength System empowers teens to explore, discover, and rearrange the world according to new interpretations of reality, ones that will help them see pathways that bring them to an unexpectedly better future.

This is the foundation for an educational approach that encourages new and meaningful discoveries. It is the foundation for an education of emergence. We embrace the entirety of our past and present and prepare ourselves for what we can't imagine that has yet to emerge. It is an orientation that allows ideas to become obsolete as they are replaced by more insightful, subtle, inclusive, and systemic ways of seeing. It allows for new contexts. It invites kids to put information and their experience together in unexpected ways. It cultivates interest and rewards discovery. Even failures, in this light, can be explored systemically and in context, and kids can find an interest in connecting the outcomes to all kinds of factors. Then they can change the momentum of failure through an authentic engagement with their own experience rather than a generally futile effort to conform to a fixed and rigid way of being. Students gain a sense of mastery over themselves and confidence that they will be able to find their way. When they start regularly saying things like this about practical challenges that arise in their lives, we can feel, as educators, that we are doing our job well:

"By using mindfulness and self-control, I was able to refrain from doing something that would probably affect me. I stepped back and realized that it wasn't worth it."

"I learned to look at things from multiple perspectives. When I am working on something tough, I can look at the benefits of whatever I'm working on to encourage myself to keep working on it. This way, something very boring or painful can become something fun."

"This class taught me how to step back and look at situations from an 'outside looking in' point of view. I learned how to make different choices and not just react."

"Overall, the Inner Strength class was very helpful. It was a good way to untangle myself from all the drama and improve my mental/emotional health."

Love & Kindness in the Classroom

If they say, who cares if one more light goes out
In a sky of a million stars?
It flickers, flickers
Who cares when someone's time runs out
If a moment is all we are?
We're quicker, quicker
Who cares if one more light goes out?
Well I do.

Linkin Park
"One More Light"

Care and kindness exercises promote positive relatedness. Teens can cultivate their capacity to care. And I've found, to my surprise, that they are happy to. One teacher described her experience in a typical inner city school this way:

I have been teaching the Inner Strength System for the last couple of years. Every class has its own challenges and its own rewards. I see these kids struggling to gain some perspective on their thoughts and feelings, and to do something that frankly, most adults I know have a hard time with—staying calm in the midst of the storm.

A few weeks ago I walked into a class for the "Love & Kindness" lesson. The students and I begin a conversation.

"Who do you take care of? Who are you supposed to be kind to?"

The answers are the same, "my mom," "my aunt," and then... surprisingly, "myself"!

We start to talk about the importance of self-care and the notions that accompany it. Self-care teaches us that we love ourselves, including all of our foibles and imperfections. Self-care builds a foundation of self-compassion and non-judgmentalism—with discrimination and goals. Self-care builds a wellspring of strength so we do not get depleted when we support others. Finally, self-care builds a community based on respect and hopefulness for the future.

I lead the kids through a Love & Kindness meditation, and the room gets quiet. The kids sit, attentive. They silently repeat to themselves the words I say aloud.

"May I be kind. May I be loving. May I be well."

I ask them to make up their own Love & Kindness phrases and finish the sentence for themselves, "May I be..."

It is quiet and peaceful in the room. The exercise is over, and the class is still. We continue with the lesson, making links between self-compassion, patience for others, and realizing one's goals. We talk about ways we practice kindness and meanness just by the thoughts we choose to pay attention to. As it comes to the end of class, I look out at the room full of students and ask, "Who would like to lead us?"

A tall young man volunteers. He walks to the front of the room. Then he asks me if there are specific words he should use. I tell him, "You've got this. Whatever you say will be good."

"OK, I want everyone to sit tall and close your eyes," he begins. "Take a few breaths, get quiet inside. Now repeat after me:

"May we love ourselves for who we are.

May we love ourselves when we are happy with ourselves.

May we love ourselves when we are disappointed with what we do.

May we love ourselves knowing we are not perfect.

May we love ourselves knowing that we are all imperfect and doing the best we can.

And may we love the world and all the people in it this way."

The stillness was palpable after the end of the meditation, and then a few moments later, the entire class burst into applause.

I could hardly move in my chair. This was by far the best Love & Kindness meditation I have ever done.

Love and kindness practices are surprisingly useful tools in the classroom. In the stillness of meditation, teens find gentleness and care they often feel far from. With practice, they gain confidence in their ability to care without exposing themselves. They gain strength in their own ability to rise up above pettiness or harshness. Teachers also benefit from this practice. We all have students who trigger us; we all have days where it's hard to let go of frustration. Practicing Love and Kindness as part of the regular activities of a conscious classroom embed this habit in us and give us regular moments to dial things down. When we wish for our students to be released from emotional and mental issues that challenge them so they can also be kind and experience kindness, it reduces our reactivity. Because of the subtle nature of influence, how we respond in any given moment can influence a child; touching them with support can alter their lives, and that life well lived may influence the course of history.

The Power of Cultural Context

The Inner Strength System incorporates lessons on big shifts in culture. Students need to know where they came from, not just personally but culturally, to understand why they react the way they do. They need to look at how history has moved to appreciate the underlying stresses and advantages our era has. One of the main ways to understand shifts in culture is to look at how our values and opportunities have changed over the last eight hundred years, from the period of early modernity into postmodernity.

Naila, a precocious and energetic sixteen-year-old, had no inhibitions talking about herself and her life. Bright and talented, she was a lead dancer in the school musical, had an internship in a youth drama program, and emitted a sparkle that made her love of the spotlight endearing. Her family history was challenging. Many of the traumatic effects of systemic poverty had touched her directly. She'd seen the inside of the foster care system, the outside of underemployment, drugs, and violence on the streets in her neighborhood. In spite of constant upheaval, she was making her way towards high school graduation in an honors curriculum.

On this day we were looking at cultural change to understand stress.

Naila squirmed in her desk until somehow she'd worked her way up to perch on the table top.

"I've had a lot of problems, I don't mind saying. I used to have a social worker but not anymore. Sometimes I just need someone to talk to. The thing is, I don't have anyone to call."

I kept teaching, my voice a little tight. No child should be so alone.

Some problems can't be solved one by one, though after that I did create a handout of call lines for the kids. That day, I set our insecure and fragmented times in context using a guided imagination exercise.

"Let's go back to a village in the early 1400s. Imagine the life then. You would know exactly what you'd wear in the morning, which shoes you'd put on, what you would eat for breakfast. If you were a boy, you'd know exactly what you'd do when you grew up. You'd follow your father's occupation, farmer or cobbler or tailor. If you were a girl you wouldn't have a profession. When you were ready to marry, you'd know the handful of eligible partners within a few villages, and your father would choose for you. Unless you were very wealthy, you wouldn't go to school. No homework! And if you were a girl you wouldn't go to school at all. When you walked through the village, everyone would know your name, what happened to you the day before. They'd know your entire family. If you had a question, you'd ask the priest or the imam or the rabbi or the village elder. They'd tell you what to do, what was right, what was wrong. They were always there to lay out your next step.

Feel the security. The stability of knowing how life was going to be, what to look forward to, what to expect.

Now, let's fast forward to our times. You wake up in the morning, late for school, tired from staying up late to do your homework. You can choose from a variety of shoes to wear to match your outfit, the new color of your hair. You take the bus listening to songs that you chose for yourself from a worldwide library of music. You are considering what profession you want to train for, where you want to live. You have a personal question; you could go for advice to your parent, guidance counselor, online search engine, crowd-sourced opinion, church or mosque or synagogue.

Feel the possibility. The creativity. The unique way you can express yourself."

When we finished, the kids exploded into insights about the pros and cons of an earlier time when life was simpler but there was far less room for individual expression.

"How many would prefer to go back to live in the 1400s and be relieved of all your homework, choice, and options?"

Not a single child raised their hands.

"How many prefer to navigate these times?"

Every hand shot up.

"Do you see that some of the confusion you have, not knowing what to choose, who to talk to, is not just your problem but is part of the way culture has evolved? We have greater freedoms, less social support. Do you see that the work of your generation and the next is to create new levels of support and connectivity that are in line with the freedoms we have today?"

Naila grinned, bright as the sun. Her frustration and isolation were now a cultural predicament that she was entrusted to solve.

Seeing from more inclusive vantage points doesn't solve all our problems. We still need to find ways to give our kids the mentorship and support they need. At the same time, it removes the personal stigma and failures and enables students to see that some of the things they feel so personally are a result of positive growth and development. There are downsides in each stage of development, and we need to build new structures of culture to make our society work and foster greater connection, support, and happiness for all. What is most important to understand about cultural development is that we exist in a historical continuum, and the outcomes right now, positive and negative, are the results of actions and beliefs set in motion a long time ago. No single individual is to blame. Leaning in, we can understand. Just as a toddler wobbles on legs strengthened through crawling, so our highly digitized and technologized age rests on strengths and skills learned from the time of the first wheel. Just as our freedoms and agency come as a result of language, urbanization, social mobility, and many other factors, so do our cultural alienation and weak social bonds.

Earlier historical stages and memories exist in our collective unconscious. All those developmental steps have left imprints in our being. We sense them sometimes and feel longing for supports from earlier eras that we have lost. Cultures continue to exist in us, as deeper archaeological layers of ourselves. Like a modern city built on top of ancient rubble, those shadows and artifacts of earlier civilizations are also layered in our individual and collective psyches. Learning how to excavate the layers and patterns of our responses and piece together the potsherds and broken alleyways of our historical past helps us make sense of the patterns and pathways available to us today. We may have buried those earlier roads under the rubble of time and generations past, but the paths we take now are still directed or defined in some way by them.

Navigating Even Bigger Factors

When we explore a worldview that includes issues too large for us to meaningfully grasp, we embrace that which we know exists but which is beyond our conceptual ability to meaningfully concretize. Usually, we take large issues and scale them down in ways that make them lose their sting. Or we avoid them entirely. Higher vantage points enable us to be with the large, the unimaginable. Bringing these issues in a meaningful way into the classroom takes them out of the shadows, makes them conscious so teens can process what is lurking over them.

Contemporary philosopher Timothy Morton looks at some of the large-scale issues that we currently have a hard time holding in our awareness. He explains how these "hyperobjects"[11] are so overarching we cannot find a place where they do not exist. We can't find anything in our experience that is not shadowed by them. He uses, as examples, global warming or the presence of nuclear waste, which is toxic for such a vast amount of time there is no place to dispose of it. As he says, there is no "away" that is far enough for us to throw nuclear waste where we could meaningfully live without its presence.

We usually think of mindfulness as a tool that helps us be with the personal issues in our lives. To see its value only in those spheres is to reduce and limit its potential. To truly work with the reality of our times and to be able to educate our teens in a way that has enough power to prepare them for life in all its wonder and threat, we have to embrace tools of awareness and perspective that are serious, potent, and positive. Some people express concern that contemplation and philosophical inquiry make us more remote. That the last thing we need is to be further removed from life, "witnessing" rather than living. They worry that broad vantage points remove us from the warm-blooded immediacy of relatedness and threaten to drop us into a cold world of ideas and abstractions. Morton's plea for us to consider the effect of large-scale issues is the very opposite. It is a plea to us to connect so that we can be in relationship with ourselves, with each other, and with our surroundings so we can respond.

CHAPTER IV

An Uncertain Age

I think I've had enough
I might get a little drunk
I say what's on my mind
I might do a little time
'Cause all of my kindness
Is taken for weakness
Now I'm FourFive seconds from wildin'
And we got three more days 'til Friday
I'm just tryna make it back home by Monday mornin'
I swear I wish somebody would tell me
That's all I want.

Rihanna, Kanye West, Paul McCartney
"FourFiveSeconds"

Interpreting Social Indicators

There is a reason our kids are experiencing extraordinary stress. They burst out in rage and frustration. They harm others. Or themselves. These are not just circumstantial issues that are simply treatable with a drug or detention. Teens aren't taught to manage the range of human emotion.[12] As much as these outbursts are the result of personal issues, they are also the accumulation of the impact from mega-trends and meta-narratives. Large-scale indicators affect our generation's consciousness whether we are aware of them or not. Some of those indicators paint the future with grim strokes. Others point to an extraordinary one, a fantastic vision, the stuff of science fiction utopias. Unless we illuminate the possibilities for students in ways that are meaningful and inspirational, the negative indicators will weigh them down.

What are some of those indicators? Can we look with an unflinching eye to get a raw sense of the unconscious pressures pressing on us and on our youth? Can we look without qualifying, without painting the bright side immediately? Not because we are pessimists or nihilists, but because those fears seep out at night from under closet doors and fill our students' dreams with worries. And they are powerless to console themselves with the skills they have. No wonder they crumble or explode. One of my students said she started using simple breathing meditation when she would wake up in terror in the night. "I could never get to sleep again before. I just couldn't calm down because it was like everything was falling on my head. Now I can make some space from it.

And I even fall back to sleep." Mindful awareness helps in practical ways. Especially when taught by educators who are able to hold their own issues without collapsing. When we can see the larger picture without recoil and hold it all in a large enough context, we'll be able to be steady for our kids. At times, we may also have strong emotional responses; sometimes those responses need to be expressed. Authentic reactions create trust. Kids crave authenticity. They crave a big heart and real care. That imparts stability.

How does this work in real time?

> *When I went into school in North Philly the day after the 2016 US presidential election to talk about the nature of mind, thought, and consciousness, I knew it was going to have to be a very different lesson. Mindfulness means being with what is. And that, particularly that week, was going to involve being OK with the unknown, the painful, the emotional, and the confusing.*
>
> *As I stood outside the high school in the misty rain, I vividly remembered a day in spring of 1968, when my second grade teacher did something that had never happened before. With misty eyes, she turned on the little black-and-white television in class. I didn't understand, but in my six-year-old pigtails, I knew it was something important. Martin Luther King had been shot. Our teacher made us bear witness and held space for us all to be with a reality beyond what our little minds could comprehend. The way she handled that moment marked my consciousness. It came back to me in vivid relief this post-election day. I wanted to be with my students and help them be with our shifting political landscape.*

I joined the bustle of changing classes in the long halls. The teacher told me some of the freshmen girls had "lost it" this morning.

"What do you mean?" I asked.

"They were frightened and crying and couldn't calm down. They had to sit in the office for hours. They were afraid of what might happen to them and their families, and they couldn't hold it together."

Approximately 97% of the students in this school come from low-income homes, 85% are African American, 5% Latino, 4% Asian, and 1% White. The school is a good academic school within a public school district. The racist, sexist, and xenophobic language tossed around in the campaign was, to these kids, a personal affront. Unfortunately, in all too real ways, it was also a personal threat.

The bell rang, and my students started to arrive. I welcomed each one as they came in, watching their faces, connecting. They seemed more than a little dazed. One asked if we were going to watch Obama's speech, which was to be broadcast shortly. That was fortunate timing. I let everyone know that up to the president's address we were going to use this time to talk together and use our meditation practice to help us manage all kinds of intense feelings, to make space, to allow everything that seems as overwhelming as it is to simply be, without becoming overwhelmed ourselves.

We meditated. The room became still. Their faces softened. If I could have held them all in one huge hug, I would have. But I just sat still, holding space for them. I drew them into the present through watching their breath, through paying atten-

tion to physical immediacy as they felt into the contact of their feet with the floor. The simple recognition of touch, of gravity, creates some grounding, especially when so many parts of ourselves don't quite know what corners of the universe we've been blown to, and the future seems so uncertain.

When we began to talk, I presented lots of questions, not answers. I wanted to hear what they were feeling. Several of these seniors had tears in their eyes.

"I just feel so sad and mad. I'm a female; how can people vote for someone who denigrates women that way?"

"I'm afraid of the racism and sexism."

"I'm afraid my friend will be deported."

"I'm afraid I won't get the financial aid to go to college."

We put all the different feelings up on the board to name them and depersonalize them. Holding the concerns in our collective awareness without melodrama, without drawing conclusions, without exacerbating fear and mistrust, and without denying the real triggers that sparked their fears.

I drew metaphors between the open space we feel in meditation and the essential non-separation of all humanity. There were increased incidences of bullying in schools when campaigning reached its fever-pitched frenzy in the last months. Reports from counselors indicated that since this political campaign, girls feel worse about themselves and their bodies. In the schools in my city, black, Jewish, LGBTQ, and Hispanic students have been taunted verbally, with scrawled messages, and even with threats of physical harm.

We talked about standing strong against divisiveness, about the universality of human suffering and delusion. We talked about the misinformed beliefs and convictions that were fueling social division and what it takes for all of us to see our fixed and rigid views. From that standpoint we are more able to respond and diffuse these incidents without vilifying other human beings. This is a tall order. To model that for our children, we must draw from our own experience of deep practice, of the essential non-separation of everything.

We cut our discussion short and turned on the live stream as President Obama appeared to address the nation. He was strong, magnanimous, and respectful. He spoke to these kids very personally. Still, several young men rolled their eyes.

"How can he say those things? Isn't he going back on everything he believes?"

We opened up the international significance of this moment, the importance of a smooth transition of power for the foundations of our own democracy and for the world's faith in peaceful governance.

We opened up what it would take for us to create bridges and unification, learning more about the lives of millions of people who had not been heard or helped by the direction America has been going. What would it mean to respect their human aspirations without condoning prejudice, threat, or meanness? This class was relatively homogeneous politically, and like many silos in our culture, these students also needed to learn to connect with those who are different, not to hide out in the shelter—or the ghetto—of the like-minded. They needed to be taught to listen beyond the rhetoric and find where they might connect and find a path as yet unknown. We talked about leaving open the possibility within this upheaval for unexpected openings, for new growth in ourselves, enhanced courage, and a different response. In times of great transition, there is potential for unanticipated ways forward.

During the discussion, one girl accusingly blurted out, "Who did you vote for?" It was so raw and unfiltered, in the way adolescents can be.

"That's disrespectful!" gasped a chorus of students. "You can't ask her something like that!"

I reassured them that if I didn't want to answer, I wouldn't. I did answer her, then moved on. In this case, my political and social sympathies dovetailed with hers. It might not have been so smooth if they had not, but I am sure the space would have held, and it would have been an opportunity to model the kind of dialogue I was just speaking to them about—to create relationship and relatedness beyond rhetoric.

In this class, the day following the US presidential election, I did my best to love the kids. To bring them space without making everything or everyone all right or all wrong. To teach them how to hold and respect their own feelings without forcing any conclusions or actions. To be. Be with themselves, with each other, and to be with an adult able to hold complexity without needing to react. I hope their experience will be one of a heart that was able to hold complexity. I hope that through this example they will become stronger, wiser, and more noble young adults.

Personal Experience & Global Shadows

We just looked at a specific example. Let's look at some of the trends that are so disheartening. That as educators we observe on a daily basis. That we need to understand and work with to create a conscious classroom. Let's start with the physical. This is the first generation where children are expected to have shorter life spans than their parents.[13] We have seen roughly 1,000 years of rising life expectancy, barring episodes of war and plague. We've been privileged with consistently lower infant mortality rates, better medicine and education, and a greater ease of living—at least up until recent decades. In America, we are now seeing the beginnings of a downslide in these trends. We are seeing a disturbing rise in childhood obesity and diabetes, stress, nutritional and environmentally related illnesses, and debilitating mental disease. In America, the huge gap in health and wellness between upper and lower socio-economic classes—which for the most part mirror the melanin spectrum (light melanin for the better outcomes, heavy melanin for the poorer outcomes)—is one of the disturbing trends and predictors of outcomes for our children.

This is the first generation where middle class children expect to earn less than their parent's generation.[14] The causes are complex, but, in broad terms, they point to a rise in corporate power and the consolidation of wealth in the small number of the über wealthy. This has all kinds of repercussions; the decrease in the effectiveness of unions and the disenfranchisement of large portions of the population are just a few. Runaway growth and unsustainable wealth bubbles are not incubators for whole-system economic health and wellness. The shrinking middle class means less stability and opportunity ahead for our youth. Whether they know the details or not, kids somehow *know* the trends. They feel it. It influences their willingness to be disciplined in school. It seeds an undergrowth of discouragement, frustration, and despair. It fuels their anxiety about college, the pressure they experience seeking financial aid. It entices them to set their eyes on a gamble, to fantasize about long shots for success. How many lower-income kids dream of being among the handful of athletes and songsters who make it mega, rather than becoming teachers or engineers or economists or designers or another profession that used to promise stability and gave youth a realistic pathway to contribute to society? Too few jobs these days offer sufficient options for a satisfying and financially sustaining career. Among the kids I teach in the inner city of Philadelphia, the poorest of the ten largest cities in America, the effect of economic disparity is all too real.

When we look at security, in spite of some analyses that show violence is decreasing overall, our perception and experience of threat is increasing. This generation is facing insidious global insecurity. Because of modern travel and the destructive power of small explosives, the potential of violence has a long arm and can reach its fingers into many crevices. War doesn't need to cover the Western world for the threat to be real for your average citizen. When rock concerts[15] and sports[16] events are no longer safe from attack; when churches[17] and political campaign stops,[18] grade schools[19] and public health departments[20] become stages for crazed outbursts of violence, every public event carries with it an underbelly of danger. When people long to gather in community, when public expressions of purpose and aspiration are ever more essential to anchor us in reality and in our human values, these violent disruptions of communal life take a significant toll on our collective unconscious. For youth who have walked too few years on this earth, this is the world they know. They do not know otherwise.

As the hype carries them deeper into fear and cynicism, educators will have to figure larger in their lives as models of an alternative and optimistic relationship to each other and to the future.

It landed for me how different my students' associations are from mine when I was in a classroom leading a silent breath meditation. It was lunchtime, and I spent our fifteen minutes of open awareness exercises listening to the laughing and playing of kids outside in the schoolyard. Their joyful raucousness made me smile. When we finished and I asked how it went, one girl shot up her hand.

"I couldn't close my eyes. I heard all the noise outside, and it reminded me of gunshots."

The week I was writing this section, my young intern teared up as I explained to her more about the rationale behind teaching inner strength for outer stability.

"The world needs this so much," she choked.

There had been another crazed assailant in a nightclub in Florida.[21] This man took forty-nine lives with him. It is harder these days to purchase a home than to amass a destructive capability that exceeds the best weaponry of great colonial empires of a few centuries ago. Our children are growing up with this reality. And with the mythology around it. The mythology that it is inevitable for our world to keep moving in this direction. The belief that humans are incorrigibly violent, competitive, callous. The conviction that kindness is an extra, not inherent to human nature. That this is progress. The jury is out on whether greed or love is the more dominant gene, though compassion and cooperation are actually leading in the most current research.[22] Our cultural narratives so influence us. Whatever story we put forward—one that believes in and moves towards greater wholeness and love, or one that moves toward greater isolation and mistrust—will have a strong influence on what will happen. Our cultural beliefs set in motion behaviors and education. Unconsciously, as we teach, we either instill a belief in humanity's inherent drive towards wickedness or towards goodness. Since the scientific jury is divided, let us choose to educate towards Love. To do that we, as educators, must authentically suspend our cynicism, tame the dragons of our own resentments, hatreds, and disbelief, and act as if goodness were trending. Then through our focus and consistent follow-through, we can see if we can make it so. Not through naïve belief, but through the conditions we create for this experiment we call our own life.

As humans, we face industrial and environmental foes that easily overpower us, both practically and psychologically. With all our industrialized ingenuity, we continue to face disasters from forces beyond our control. Even though in our urbanized environments we usually feel far from nature's furies, the wilds are not far from us. In 2005, Hurricane Katrina left 1,833 dead and flooded 800,000 homes in Louisiana and Mississippi.[23] Just five years later a massive earthquake in Haiti took the lives of 316,000 people. And five years after that, in 2015, 8,000 lives were lost in an earthquake in Nepal. Add to that changes in weather patterns that affect us with floods, hurricanes, droughts, heat waves, and record snow and cold. Birds and fish are being affected, too, by toxic waterways, overfished shorelines, and pesticides burning the insides of whales on the other side of the ocean.[24] There have been changes in migration patterns and birds forgetting verses of their birdsong.[25] We are experiencing the closing in of environmental degradation. That kind of pressure on other species can't help but affect our consciousness. Even though toxins are directly linked to effects on human health, still, urban developers build for short-term profits, not long-term balance. They cut corners and neglect integration with the plant-based environment or with community regeneration.

I recently testified at the city education budget hearing about the value of trauma-informed mindfulness programs in schools. Before my testimony there was a press conference with a doctor from Physicians for Social Responsibility, several council members, and a woman with a four-year-old child whose level of lead was so high[26] she was hospitalized and receiving injections every two hours. The problem stemmed from both her rental apartment and from her school, where the bathrooms had signs for the kids too young to be able to read saying, "Do not drink the water." Lead poisoning is directly linked to long-term neurological damage, affecting IQ and learning as well as bones, teeth, and kidneys, irreversibly, for a lifetime. These are hard facts to take in. We cannot avoid the interconnected nature of incidents like these and the psychological toll it takes on our ability to feel safe and at home in our world. These physiological threats and the fear of harmful influences beyond our control diminish the ability of the youth of today to be good stewards of our world when they mature. These issues need a resilient outlook as well as practical solutions.

Inner strength and resilience provides us with a wellspring of upliftment so we are not consumed by fears and sorrow that arise in response to the dangers of our age. As we have seen, from the perspective of interdependence and process—of co-dependency and co-arising—from the recognition of the continuous motion and unfolding of life, *everything influences everything else.* Everything is in flow. Everything is connected, from the smallest beetle to the giant elephants on the savannahs. When other life forms experience fear, threat, and suffering from toxic water and foods, or from warm or cool temperatures, they cannot withstand, or from the loss of habitat, we all feel it. It is entirely possible that that visceral recoil or pain doesn't just occur at the level of species that we see react (like our dogs or cats) but among trees, networks of mushrooms, perhaps even entire soil cultures.[27] Our children are growing up at a time when the existential fear of so many species in the great chain of life is heightened and valid. To think we're not affected by that, in one way or another, is not logical when we look closely. Once we take into consideration how we are affected by the dangers around us, it makes sense that our cultural angst is both the result of factors we can name and blame within a five-mile radius of our homes and also of fears that come from increasingly frenetic ripples in the chain of being.

Underlying our social malaise is something more systemic, a trend so large there is virtually nothing we do that doesn't reference (or ignore) it, that isn't influenced by its changes, or doesn't yearn for or bargain for some solution. That trend is large-scale climate change. Global warming may be one of the most important undocumented causes of the social, psychological, and practical unrest in this generation. Our generation is experiencing the greatest increase of weather-related changes in 15,000 years. This can't help but influence our experience and pressure our psyches in conscious or unconscious ways. One way this is brought home to inner city school cultures is through human migration. Through refugee children sitting in the next desk over. Climate change underlies instability in so many nation-states. The UN currently estimates there are twenty million climate refugees.

If you add climate refuges to those families fleeing war and civil unrest, we see a picture of flux and upheaval that is hard to take in from the relative stability of US city neighborhoods and public schools. The reality is that the world our kids live in is facing the greatest mass migration since World War II. Fleeing from a variety of causes, from climate-related agricultural failure to religious and ethnic rivalry to geopolitical energy and mineral grabs to national and ethnic conflicts, approximately 65 million or 1 out of every 100 humans on earth are refugees.[28] Uprooted from home, family, tribe, culture, and language, they carry with them few possessions and mementos on their back. They carry in their minds' eye pictures no one should have had to see. While we relate to these issues as if they are pictures from news broadcasts affecting former beachfront resort areas[29] in the Mediterranean sea, still, they directly touch our schools, and those memories of classmates affect all of our students.

We act as if cultures can naturally assimilate, blending into the milieu of the times, like sand castles dissolving back into the shore. But in reality, our human family needs its roots and long-lived histories. Our family structure, our network of communities, our histories, and our connection with our ancestors, our roots, and our stories are essential for our deep well-being. Most times unintentionally, but irreparably, large-scale social and economic forces that move invisibly through nations leave behind a changed world in their wake. These forces separate a people from their land, from their familiar environment and gathering places. They scatter a neighborhood to tent camps and foreign shores, remove the men through incarceration or conscription, leave villages and neighborhoods vulnerable and fragmented.

We see some of those who have been displaced from their homes in our cities, first-generation immigrants mixed in the schools and in neighborhoods of poverty. While the numbers that arrive in any individual school may be few, the sorrow and aspiration they bring with them is the tip of a funnel whose mouth is open to so much tragedy. Memories from frightening upheaval come with the children into our schools halfway around the world. Impressions carried by youth whose lives have been uprooted and disrupted, who are at a loss without their familiar stabilizing social networks.[30] To fit in with their peers, children try to forget their past. New friends have no idea what their peers have witnessed. Children grow. Traumas get buried in a collective unconscious like a pit of bones. Silent or spoken, this dissonance becomes part of the classroom's common space, our collective school consciousness. Unless we recognize the ghosts and shadows and find ways to embrace the un-embraceable, our children will have to work through the repercussions of their experiences on their own.

We talk about the psychological wounds children experience when their parents' generation has suffered a trauma or addiction. Lois Wilson, wife of Bill Wilson, co-founder of Alcoholics Anonymous, organized a path for children to work out the effects of their traumas and secondary stresses from their parents' addictions through programs called Al-Anon and Alateen.[31] Extensive research has been done on the psychological trauma experienced by children of Holocaust survivors. In the United States, for over 398 years the African American population has seen its family unit stretched and separated, pulled apart like seedlings in a tray, to be replanted in new soil or tossed aside. Some individuals have made it, grown hardy in spite of the upheaval; far more have languished without a stable root bed. Most have borne the scars of traumatic exploitation beyond the scope of this book to address. Over the last fifteen years, Dr. Joy DeGruy has put together a groundbreaking body of work she calls Post Traumatic Slave Syndrome (PTSS).[32] DeGruy identifies, with meticulous research, the fabricated basis of racial differences as we have come to know them. She connects the dots between these false stereotypes and systemic limited expectations that hold black and brown children back and limit their access to opportunities their white counterparts receive. She links rough behavior within black families and harsh disciplinary trends in schools to habits of segregation grown up over hundreds of years. She looks at trauma passed down from generation to generation as they affect our kids today.

While our classrooms are not designed to remedy these issues, as conscious educators we cannot avoid their effect on the kids we are teaching. We increasingly depend on ways to help students help themselves. Contemplative practices and empathy building are effective, teachable, and easy to practice. During practice, teens from a variety of cultures and experiences can create a collective environment that fosters their well-being. These practices can create a paradigm shift in our educational system, a shift in what we teach and how we teach it. Whether our students are new refugees, children of parents with substance issues, or twentieth-generation descendants from slavery,[33] our youth will be more resilient and less likely to fall prey to the shadow of their experiences or to secondary stresses when practices that support their well-being are in place in the classroom.

The Inner Strength System gives both educators and students resilience and perspective to be able to hold space for these traumatic issues, even if we don't know the specifics. It provides tools that accommodate extremes in our students' experience within the learning environment without unnecessary distraction from the learning that needs to take place.

Contemplative practices provide ballast. Shared silence and kindness exercises create an environment of empathy and resolution, without a teacher needing to address issues that are beyond our skill set or the boundaries of a classroom to address. When we are steady and provide an environment of ease and support, without delving into specific experiences and without pretending that our students all have an equal set of memories, we will make the classroom an environment of acceptance, warmth, and security. Sharing mindful space together establishes a touchstone of support amidst unspoken emotional turbulence. It allows those students who need more specific care to find ways to reach out on their own for additional support.

My generation grew up with images of famine in Ethiopia and exhortations of "Eat your dinner; there are starving children in Africa." We saw the first huge musical benefit—humanitarian George Harrison's Concert for Bangladesh—which led to Band Aid, Live Aid,[34] and a host of other artists giving young people a way to come together and channel their privilege, generosity, and their care. When I was 18, hitchhiking with my best friend across Europe (in those days, before the weapons craze, it was still possible to backpack with abandon), we took a boat from Tel Aviv to Athens and then made our way across the turquoise Mediterranean to Spetsai, with linen-white sand and fluorescent algae that sparkled gold when we swam under the moonlight. Spetsai was an island on the other side of Athens, some 350km west of Lesbos. We considered Lesbos too touristy in 1980, too filled with luxury villas and families of four, too tame for our youthful adventures. The island of Lesbos is now bedraggled and weary, its beaches stained with the shadow of souls washed up, infants and mothers, medical students and chemists, teachers and grandfathers clutching at hope, in desperation over what has happened to their world. When we hear analyses of that area, we rarely hear about the roots and the value of Iraqi, Irani, or Syrian history, of the area that once was the cradle of civilization, that once held the world's largest library. Syria is considered to have the oldest organized library, some 4,500 years old, while Iraq's library of Ashurbanipal contained some twenty thousand volumes almost 2,700 years ago.[35] Countries from this most troubled region produced some of the most advanced mathematics, the most erudite literary culture that formed the foundations for most of the modern nations in the world. We rarely build on the contributions from the people who lived on that spot on our one blue planet.

We have benefitted so much from those cultures. That legacy and pride has all but disappeared under the rubble and the racism of the last couple of centuries and the amnesia of today. Do students today still create poster-board projects mapping out the cradle of civilization in uncertain strokes? Do they still wonder at the minds that could envision such great cultures with so much mathematical, literary, medical, and engineering complexity, even while the lives they led were almost as simple as 50,000 years earlier? Fire and the wheel a million years ago[36] were great advancements, but the leap of the mind in ancient Iraq in 660 BCE took humanity a profound and important step forward. Can we educate in context to pull out the value and the connections?

The Inner Strength System works with a perspective on large-scale cultural change, to unearth these issues and their impacts in a broad way. Its goal is not all-important individual therapeutic work but rather creating shared understanding and collective classroom space that can embrace and contextualize these issues for better understanding between everyone. Seeing the evolution of culture reveals common threads and influences between Iraqis and Americans, between regions of the world currently at odds. We are so interconnected and so dependent on each other. Building pathways of appreciation and knowledge creates a felt connection, a touch point to the "other." The value of seeing in context can't be underestimated. Educating students to see the present in light of much greater swaths of history changes how we see the past and the present. History becomes not a single chain of events but a current in which we are all appearing like foam on the surface. Putting all this together, the positive and the concerning, helps us find ways to move forward. Teaching our students about actions and reactions, rises and falls of great civilizations and connections with the past, can re-contextualize how entire races think about themselves. In the series *Africa's Great Civilizations*,[37] Harvard historian Henry Lewis Gates Jr. describes the emotional moment when he visited the great African library of Timbuktu, founded in the fourteenth century. This library held hundreds of thousands of books, mostly written by African authors who worked in the city. Africans came from all over the continent to mine its riches. "I grew up learning that Africans never wrote books," Gates confessed. "Yet here was this astonishing treasure trove.... I felt incredible pride and vindication."

Without our cultural history, we have no roots. Without roots, we can blow this away and that in just a puff of breeze. Without the weight of history, we are like the fairy-tale piglets living in our houses of straw that the wolf of war just huffs and puffs and blows into a pile of chaos. How are we going to find our way through systemic institutionalized racism and the devastating cultural issues without roots, knowledge, history, context—and space to hold it all?

Our personal histories affect us. Our cultural histories affect us. I came of age during the Watergate hearings, and I'll never forget that summer, growing out of childhood and experiencing new personal freedoms coupled with the televised display of lies and criminal activity at the highest level of power in my country. It changed me. And it marked my generation. These days, the dishonesty, vengefulness, emotionalism, and power-grabbing by public figures are also imprinting on young minds and shaping young character. These are not the influences I would wish to see as an educator. In response, I find myself more and more frequently evoking role models who stood for higher ideals, talking about the challenges they faced, and the inner strength that gave them fuel and resilience. The personal examples help—Nelson Mandela, Mother Theresa, Dalai Lama, Martin Luther King. To help students internalize these examples and feel that those qualities are within reach, I emphasize the values and the source of moral courage, rather than the individuals, as inspiring as they are.

President George Bush famously called us to build a "kinder, gentler nation." That type of nation rests on the health, well-being, and happiness of its individuals. Well-being is the result of a variety of factors, which are increasingly being measured around the world. The experiments with Bhutan's Gross National Happiness Index and innovative classroom training show that educating for well-being increases student academics as well as personal ease. Well-being includes being able to handle complexity. The Inner Strength System presents an alternative to combative argumentation. It teaches exercises that promote trust in human capacities and the recognition of our shared desire for connection, belonging, and love. Teaching teens how to settle into themselves, how to identify the influences pushing them this way and that, and giving them ways to find their own authentic responses and the courage to be true to themselves empowers them. With that stability they can pursue their own higher aspirations. That's why these tools are potentially such positive social disruptors. As educators then, we release our kids' capacity to care and let them experience support from feeling connected, in sync with the flow of their experience, and able to hold challenge.

Working with Historical Levers

To help our students see in context, we are called to assimilate the historical levers on which their experience pivots. That is an aspect of the conscious interpretation of history. Context enables us to better see how some decisions have a long arm reaching into the future, affecting "unto the tenth generation," and not always for the good. That perspective is essential; it is the foundation to teach students to care about the momentum they create. How, once set in motion, certain flows cannot be stopped or reversed. Adjusting course may not be possible, and history will unfold in the direction it was propelled because a new sluice shoot to change a negative course may not be able to be opened in time. Such is the delicacy of cultural momentum.

The context I am advocating helping students understand includes the long trail of human history and also extends to our universe's early history. It reaches back into time before woman and man walked upright on the earth. It assimilates the momentum of history as life has grown and evolved. This progression leaves a mark almost as a cellular memory, one that lives in the code of human beings, not just in any particular cell or DNA sequence. When teens learn to perceive what is known as "deep time," this 13.7-billion-year trajectory, they can begin to see how the universe "talks" to them, not metaphysically, but simply in how deeply influences from the environment affect them. Our liver and eyelash may not "talk" to each other, but they form elements of a whole that have a unity which we only see because of our ability to relate to the person contained by a skin. Taking in the broader environment lets a teen see the connection or "unity" between their eyelash and their liver. It also allows them to connect the dots between systems and influences. It opens them to see reality utterly differently than they have ever considered before. It allows for unexpected, emergent possibilities. How? A student sees that there are different ways of perceiving that shift their interaction with the world. They allow themselves to be with what is, rather than avoiding or pushing away. It can be frightening and unfamiliar, but contemplative tools are also supportive. That is also why learning how to self-reflect, calm, and re-contextualize—as a matter of course for our educational world—can be a game changer.

The Plight & Prospect of Urban Schools

A variety of factors in our favor at this particular moment in history support the promotion of depth and contextual training. Some are positive and some are negative. The picture they make up is at once threatening, encouraging, and galvanizing.

Let's take the example of my home city to see how the confluence of issues and policies may be making this time ripe for cultural and educational change. While the specifics may vary from state to state, the scale of the trends and the direction they set are illustrative of currents and priorities in our increasingly silo-ed and divided culture. Without a systemic view that gives us a felt sense of care for the overall health and balance of our culture, it will be hard to chart a clear way through. As you'll see, the complexity and intransigence of urban issues is necessitating more simple, albeit profound, tools to deal with children's well-being.

In Philadelphia, where the Inner Strength System was first released, you can see the perfect storm, which makes educating, in the system as we have known it, difficult. In this city, which is hardly unique among large American cities, educational coffers have been gutted for years by failed or limited policy. Pressure to bring industry into the state led to short-sighted incentives with the natural gas industry.[38] These incentives opened the way to toxic extraction techniques. These techniques had their own effect on the surrounding environment, and to couple insult with injury, the incentives sent the profits out of state to shareholders without retaining a meaningful income to fund state needs, especially in education. Other states handled this differently and retained revenue and benefits. Changing demographics put pressure on lawmakers to make large cuts in the education budgets in the more densely populated urban areas to presumably make funding fair across the state. The result? Philadelphia's school budget was slashed by $198 million in 2011–12. These cuts represented a twenty-percent decrease, while the rest of the state's schools received a four-percent increase in educational funding.[39] The urban area reductions led to a fiscal chasm too deep to heal.

The short-term solution? The city turned to private and charter schools. Meant to be independent of state funds, these schools were purported to be more efficient, more effective, run like businesses. The reality? Charter schools, by and large, couldn't support themselves and depended on funds from the already-stretched education budget, taking away from the public schools. Because they were each independently run, individual administrative and procurement offices added layers of cost and inefficiency. Unable to staff, train, and equip themselves on their own, charter schools began pressuring for more funding from the city. Some closed, leaving students with instability and a sense of abandonment. Then the school district, with few funds for capital improvements, started closing and selling off neighborhood schools to property developers. In their efforts to offload expenses and to offload the pressure of fixing failing schools riddled with violence and dysfunction, they cut deals that were rarely in favor of the district. The loss? To the neighborhoods, the students, and the sense of belonging. That level of uprooting has had long-term effects on students as well as the delicate cultural meshwork that makes cities thrive.

From a distance, it's easy to feel dispassionate towards the closing of failed schools. Expensive, unresponsive, hardly places where quality learning takes place. It's not easy to feel sentimental about the closing of a structure you would hardly want to visit, let alone teach at, and one that you wouldn't want to send your children to. But from the neighborhood view, when you see the children whose local school is closing with no replacement, the weight of failure and abandonment lies heavy on young minds and hearts. The feeling of being discarded, irrelevant, with the moniker "closed," casts a pall on their future.[40]

Let's look a little further at the financial pressures within the schools and the comparison to another industry that seems to be a pipeline for too many urban kids. The average salary of high school advanced placement and honors teachers in the public school system in Philadelphia is $62,784.[41] It rose by 23 percent in two decades. The salary of a top private prison corporation's C-level executive was $6 million in 2012. In the last thirty years, state and local expenditures for education doubled, while state and local expenditures of corrections quadrupled from $17 billion to

$71 billion per year. Huge investments—and profits—that are not leading toward a future we look forward to. The whole issue of wasted human potential and mass incarceration is an important inquiry unto itself. Without going into that in detail, we can see that with investment patterns like this, it is not an accident that the quality of public education is in the shape it is in or that our national results are declining at the rate they are. Poor education is not an issue isolated to preschoolers, middle schoolers, or high schoolers in specific zip codes. Poor education affects a lifetime, expectations for the next generation, and their generation of children. It affects the readiness of our workforce to meet the future and the level of service we experience now. It affects the creative capital of our nation and the quality of life we can expect to experience as this generation matures.

When we see that the school allocation per student is $12,570 per year, while the allocation for juvenile detention per teen is $148,767 per year,[42] we see where attention and trends lie. Expediency, even at a higher price tag, has radically affected our outlook on urban education and urban poverty and on policy. Character-building and relationships take time and personal availability, and that seems to ask more of us as a culture than we are willing to fund. Invisible to us, the lens of industrialization has led us to bias a conveyor-belt approach over the interpersonal, relational education that leads to the flowering of a child's potential, to a happy, more mature adult. Whether by design or by default, those institutions that stand to earn the most profits for shareholders—shareholders who will never partake of the services they are making their monies from—are the ones towards which our urban educational model is increasingly leaning.

We say kids are our future, which literally they are since they will run all the institutions and populate the workplace that cares for both our world and us as we age and pass on. And we say that education is the best predictor of child outcomes. Yet it's clear that the best of our time, energy, and financial resources are not going into our urban public schools. Since we are dealing with such infrastructure dysfunction and systemic confusion about how to remedy these issues, educational hacks are all the more important. Ways to connect with kids now—before budget enhancements, neighborhood improvements, or school reform take place. Ways that are cost-efficient, easily delivered, and that empower the students to continue to grow strong on their own. Since we don't have a single solution or approach, I believe the most powerful way we can respond is to let loose a generation of students who can think creatively and systemically, in a broad context, and with real care about the long-term effects of the steps we take now. With a system as broad yet as supportive as the Inner Strength's contemplative and integral-thinking model, we can, in a short space of time, create educational environments that bring about heart, shared camaraderie, and positive aspiration. And when we empower kid's potential, who knows what they will be able to do.

CHAPTER V

Change Agents in Our Midst

Chicago nights they stay on the mind
But I write many lives, they lay on these lines
Wavin' signs of the times, many say the grind's on the mind
Shorties blunted-eyed and everyone wanna rhyme
Bush pushing lies, killers immortalized
We got arms but won't reach for the skies

Waiting for the Lord to rise,
I look into my daughter's eyes
And realize I'm a learn through her
The Messiah might even return through her
If I'm a do it, I gotta change the world through her…

Walk like warriors, we were never told to run
Explored the world to return to where my soul begun
Never looking back or too far in front of me
The present is a gift and I just want to be.

Common
"Be"

Learning in the New Collectives

Youth today recognize in some visceral way the sea-change we are in the midst of. Without organizing into any great Occupy movement, without voicing their direction to themselves, let alone to their peers, they are making decisions and responding in ways that reflect this awareness. In many, that response is a creative outpouring of new ways to organize, connect socially, do business, create art. Because they are so immersed in the current of change, they don't necessarily see how new what they are doing is. But from a half step back, we can see that these youngsters are literally evolving the way we do things.

Have you noticed the micro-enterprises started by a couple of twenty-somethings? Their structure, systems, and materials sourcing are different than the norm. They follow a set of self-fashioned ideals, and those motives have a distinct effect on the economy, on working collaborations, and on consumer interconnectedness. Have you become aware of the urban farming initiatives in Philadelphia and Detroit that are greening vacant lots for restorative aesthetics as well as for food? These are creative responses to poverty and food ghettos, to chemicalized and processed foods devoid of nutrition and that contribute to a variety of illness.[43] Innovations like these arise from the circumstances of our times. They carry with them the coding for new ways of structuring our cities, our families, our health, our joys. I've been amazed by the vision of some off-the-grid energy and design projects just waiting for digital printing to reach a more sophisticated capacity so they can scale. Most of us have contributed to no-interest, no-return loans, the new *crowdsourcing* or collective financing. If anyone had said, "Strangers will one day give you money so you can follow your dream," it would have sounded farcical. But crowdsourcing is now a noun in Merriam-Webster's dictionary. New connectivity in the digital age has enabled new forms of human friendship. We are now touched by the lives of strangers way beyond our kith and kin. Through the "gofundme" movement, individuals are making possible everything from tuition for a teaching certificate to bike rides across Central America, from medical treatments too expensive for the child's family to the restoration of villages in Nepal following a catastrophic earthquake, from classroom resources to my own school mindfulness program. Donations of a few dollars from friends, family, and like-minded others are giving creative youth a step up. Larger projects are enabled by many small gestures, empowering youth to believe it is possible to reach beyond their current circumstances in a nonlinear trajectory. Youth are learning they can contribute, friend, and explore beyond their means. We are connected. And we do help one another.

Millennials are pushing forward with a new culture of sharing, changing our relationship as iconic America car owners to the way we now share our own homes and beds. Who would have thought we would welcome strangers into our houses for the weekend or catch rides with someone from the other side of town? From share cars and bikes like Zipcar and Indego, rideshares like Lyft and Uber, houseshares like Airbnb, Office-shares like WeWork, we are becoming used to new models of ownership, use, and entrepreneurship. This culture of sharing is changing how small segments of our economy may work moving forward. It is spawning social entrepreneurship and other ways to connect, collaborate, and create fluidity of relationships and of purpose.

It is our job as conscious educators to welcome and encourage this sea-change of connectivity and innovation. We can equip our students with tools that enable them to chart their own destiny and change all of ours for the better. This kind of quiet revolution in the structure of our teaching and students' learning takes away isolation and disconnectedness. It allows teens to surf the waves of discovery and work with distributed support structures that can catch their fall. This focus on the individual *within* the collective is a model that empowers a student's autonomy without cutting him or her off from interconnections that fuel possibility.

Add that collective way of learning and doing to digital and information capacities, and we see teens empowered to innovate at an extraordinary rate. Most of the gadgets that were science fiction when I first saw them while religiously watching *Star Trek* after school with my best friend when I was in fourth grade are now every day appliances.[44] We talk to our cars. We have video conversations across the world in the palms of our hands. We translate almost any language on demand. We program music to our likes and discover artists we never knew but that we are pretty much guaranteed to love. Are we educating for *this* world—the world of options and access—or the world of the 1950s?

To take advantage of the trends that have taken root so quickly we need to bring them to the forefront of our consciousness—in context. Conscious educators need to recognize what is emerging and what forces will resist that emergence. We will also need to shift our focus and jettison some of the more restrictive and outmoded structures of our education system. We would do well to question everything from the schedules of our school days to the shape of the desks kids sit on. We may have to lead the way from the classroom, for large-scale bureaucratic systems change slowly and are often too removed from the students' joy and learning to see the rewards of real change.

Youth have the most uncanny ability to learn. Reaching that insatiable curiosity and willingness to experiment without limit yields results well more interesting and advanced than the test-ridden pathway most students currently tread. Sugata Mitra's "hole in the wall" kids from India, for example.[45] These illiterate, non-English speaking, non-technologically savvy kids learned how to use a computer without *any* guidance. The computer was set in a hole in a wall in a remote village with a hidden camera recording what happened. The kids taught themselves enough English to understand instructions and wove two hundred words into their vocabulary. Their relationships and curiosity produced remarkable group learning. A sixteen-year old Dutch teenager, who loves sea diving, conceived of an idea to clear fifty percent of plastics from the Great Pacific Garbage Patch, the world's major ocean trash site, in just five years. It's a simple concept, using the ocean's currents to funnel large plastics against a cleanup system. This system catches the toxic plastics before they break apart into even more harmful microplastics, which are ingested by species up and down the food chain. A sixty-person organization sponsored by the Government of the Netherlands and overseen by major scientists is setting about to do so, with the young man at the helm.[46]

The resilience of the teens I teach is nothing short of extraordinary. With the physical insecurity of real poverty, the harshness of the neighborhoods around them, the discouragement from some authority figures, stereotyping in the media, and the neglect from overburdened or absent caretakers, one would think that they would hardly make it past the tender ages of early childhood. That their curiosity and thirst to learn carries them through to maturity and higher education I feel is nothing short of heroic. That we've allowed our schools to devolve to such a degree is nothing short of shameful. Though we might all agree with the dysfunction of our public school system, our challenge as educators is to resist the temptation to dwell on blame. Blame won't lift our vantage point towards a holistic and more forward-looking altitude. It won't fill us with the energy we need to introduce new thinking. What helps is to hold all the facts, along with our care for our students' future, and see what emerges. We rarely sit still long enough to let a new possibility make itself known out of that space and stillness. The facts are tough. The fact of social dysfunction and decay. The fact of child resiliency and curiosity. The fact of alienation and broken family ties over generations. The fact of new ways people are connecting. The fact of institutionalized bias and mediated assumptions and the fact of increasing tolerance for gender fluidity and personal expression. The fact of mass incarceration and the trend towards wealth consolidation and the fact of cell phone cameras making the hidden public and empowering the disenfranchised. The fact of heightened urbanization and distance from our biophilic nature and the fact of the slow food movement and the recognition of the multi-dimensions of health and wellness.

The tools of mindful awareness and contextual thinking enable us to take in the enormity of these issues without sentimentalizing, without fury, and without caving in from the implications of what we see. It enables us to see the bias towards life in the human spirit and through that begin to imagine a way forward. Changing or enlarging the framework we use enables our students to turn their relationship to their experience upside down. They become interested in their experience rather than victimized by it. By shifting the vantage point from where they are looking, youth can flip from an experience of overwhelm to one of curiosity. Letting loose the reins that control the path of learning opens up the classroom. Bringing youth together in ways they can safely think freely, connect with each other, and organize along non-traditional lines, we give them the space to solve seemingly intractable problems. Entrusting the next generation to find emergent solutions is essential for a teen's self-respect, and for our shared future.

Sparking Curiosity

The Inner Strength System is a set of philosophical views and practical exercises. And it's more than that. Teaching how to see systemically and integrally is teaching a way to *be* in the world. Once learned, it is self-administered, without props, medication, or oversight. And once internalized, it is applied without effort. It becomes an inner touchstone that helps students navigate in the midst of the fog and storms. At a time when inflammatory rhetoric seems to be the tenor of public discourse, be it in politics or media, seeing systemically and integrally is a salve that spreads evenness, equanimity, understanding, complexity, and a common humanity. It implicitly and at times explicitly reminds us of a universality, a connection with each other and with the plant, animal, and planetary world.

As tempting as the contemporary diatribe is, the issues we're facing are more complex than polemical left and right positions. Even the fact that we're in this war of left and right is part of a cultural movement which, when better understood, gives us the chance of bypassing it to instead listen for that new refrain that speaks to a more cohesive and unified perspective.

The urgent need for integrative and contemplative tools in the classroom, in large part, comes from the outgrowth of poverty, economic disenfranchisement, the invisible but systematic lines that bind and limit movement, hope, possibility, and reality. The traumas and the undercurrents of disease and fear are way beyond a teacher's ability to address. Without the skills, time, and solutions, teachers struggle to teach and inspire. It's hard to reach kids through a wall of static and fuzz. The idea that we can transform our educational environment and truly support students without working to articulate a new and more inclusive way of seeing is bound to lead to frustration and failure.

Pushing the lever of curiosity by connecting students to the big patterns in history can take the heavy weight of dysfunction and set it in such a big context that it becomes part of the stuff of our great evolutionary unfolding. It becomes another epoch in history that we struggle to see in context, from within the midst of it, as it's occurring.

As educators, when we work to see all these forces in context, when we view our students as products of the influences of great movements of history, as effects from millions of years of physiological formation and brain chemistry, of two thousand generations driven by the human thirst to know the unknowable, we see trends and our contemporary struggles differently. Psychology taught us to look at our personal or familial history to explain behavior. That's been useful, and in its time it was revolutionary. But now it is not a large enough time frame for us to get perspective. That view too often stigmatizes children and families in ways that just don't take into account the reality of large-scale forces of history and their effects on us now.

Viewing our current situation from the perspective of potential, looking at the human thirst to discover and create, valuing our drive to explore the edges of the known, draws from a powerful, mysterious, and unpredictable source: the source of innate human curiosity. From earliest history, dating back some 140,000 years, humans have created abstract representations, art, and ceremony, stretching out an ancient hand to touch the ineffable. When we give children the experience of a creative source by letting them rest in stillness and experience rejuvenation, when we point them to explore the qualities of being aware rather than the objects that they are aware of, we direct them to explore the nature of human consciousness.

In one of the high schools where I teach, a renovation project is underway. The building was made to hold over 1,500 students and has just 500 walking the halls. The once thriving neighborhood school with illustrious alumnae, including Chubby Checker, Frankie Avalon, and Brandeis University founder Israel Goldstein, is one that neighborhood kids shun. In the 2012 school year it was still on the Philadelphia Board of Education's "Persistently Dangerous School" list.[47]

In the class I taught, the freshmen were both young for their age and conditioned by experience. I'd periodically find one young man watching cartoons on his iPhone while another would throw in references to guns just to see how I'd react. Teaching them to let go and let some space into their experience, while holding the space for them so they could relax and be safe for a short period, I could feel the undercurrents of self-protectiveness, disinterest, and continuous distraction.

Initially, they had a hard time really paying attention to some of the more subtle aspects of the mindful contemplation. But I kept at it. Just being with them week after week, interested in their experience, supportive of their innate intelligence, and respecting their space and boundaries.

On the last day of the year, I wanted to leave them with enough to be able to gain some respite from peer pressure and the hotheads of summer streets, so we did a review of our mindfulness tools and when to use them. Then I challenged them to think about what awareness is. I told them about experiments where people who were blind from birth were taken into a hallway filled with obstacles. The experiments showed that blind people can navigate their way, as if "seeing" the objects from the inside of their awareness. One bright and highly disinterested student looked up, curious. Then we talked about the bending of time and space. Of how certain experiments show that quantum objects, like photons, don't choose whether they show up as a wave or as particles until they are observed.[48] *This was a little too much for them. Some of them turned back to their phones or began combing their hair, a seemingly endless teen preoccupation. I kept sharing these wild scientific theories, connecting the dots with our mindfulness work.*

In mindfulness, we create space; we ground ourselves enough to be present while endlessly exploring our experience to be able to have breakthrough insights about the nature of awareness. By watching one of the most universal aspects of human life, the breath, we cultivate inner strength, confidence, and curiosity in life. We talked about how seeing our experience freshly by focusing on small sensations in the body alleviates boredom. It wakes our senses up. When I finished and wished them a good summer, almost all had turned back to talk to each other, text from their phones, or take a catnap on their desks. Only a few said goodbye or thank you.

But I heard later, from the city director of schools, that the teachers in that school requested that we expand the program. They saw a big change in the kids. They got along better with each other. They were more supportive, interested, and calm. They helped moderate the climate in the classroom for other students. In short, they were newly connected to their own thirst for real learning.

Pointing kids to explore unanswerable questions about things like the nature of human consciousness peaks their curiosity. It's the kind of challenge that gets their juices going. Adolescence is a stage that doesn't really believe in "can't." The mystery of mindful awareness and contextual thinking perfectly excites their developing brains.

Trauma-Informed Mindfulness A Humble Approach

Exploring the nature of consciousness is called the "hard question" of neuroscience by research expert David Chalmers, founder of the University of Arizona Science of Consciousness Conference. The soft question being mapping the parts of our brain that are aware of various emotions and reflexes and other very sophisticated questions. That hard question is the how and why we have developed awareness. It involves looking at awareness itself, rather than looking at the objects that we are aware of. When we look at the field of consciousness and see the universality of awareness, that there is nothing we can perceive or know that is outside of awareness, we immediately depersonalize our experience. It's not just "my" experience; it becomes experience knowing itself. We enlarge the frame within which we are viewing all the injustices and dysfunction we just discussed. When we create some space or objectivity on *what* we are seeing, we are better able to understand *how* we can most constructively interpret these facts and find our role in a solution, take a step forward. Some people argue that we can't set the bar so high, that it's unrealistic to expect most urban high school students to tackle subtle questions that doctoral candidates in philosophy of mind struggle with. But I like to present these questions to them. I challenge them with issues that are deliberately hard to ponder. These questions make them wrinkle up their noses, let their ear buds fall out of their ears, and perk up with curiosity. We all start to have fun. Education that challenges pulls out kids' innovation and imagination. They feel a sense of confidence when they are entrusted with the hard questions, not the ones they have to study for, but the ones that no one has answers to. It draws out a very different quality in them.

You can see that exploring the field of awareness in which all these issues arise radically changes the vantage point of exploration. Teens can do this. In fact they love it, because it creates an altered perception of the world without drugs or other mind-bending experiences. We bend experience by changing our frame of reference. It requires focus, subtlety, and openness, all qualities that teens need to cultivate to be successful in their academic pursuits.

What do these advanced questions have to do with trauma-informed education? Interestingly, a lot. The Inner Strength System is an orientation. We as educators meet our kids where they are and lift them up. A trauma-informed approach and toolkit are much needed, and thankfully, educators are rapidly changing how they respond to children who have seen or experienced things no one should have to and who understandably suffer from the disturbing impact. Mindfulness is increasingly being brought into schools to help students to center, be calm, and return to the present when disturbing memories from the past come to their minds or triggers get tripped and they react disproportionately to the situation in front of them. It is troubling to see youngsters so badly affected, and the call for love and understanding couldn't be greater.

Children who suffer extreme anxiety or post-traumatic stress from witnessing violence must be responded to with care and sensitivity. While mindful activities can be helpful, *they are not a blanket panacea.* Mindful activities can trigger anxiety. They can bring repressed memories to the surface or activate other triggers. All educators must take care, be very sensitive, cautious, and conservative when working with children who have experienced trauma. Educators must also be well versed with contemplative tools themselves to be able to recognize subtle discomfort and signs of unwholesome anxiety that indicate a need to stop the exercise. That being said, we want to do all that we can to help a student heal and normalize without solidifying an identity of victimhood, damage, or inadequacy. Our own contemplative practice, which lets us tap into an ultimately resilient aspect of our humanity—the human will to live—can guide us to affirm that vital life force in our students, all the while keeping our eye out for any extra support that might be called for.

You can see how curiosity begins to re-emerge when students are left unpressured but presented with intriguing tools that are affirming, healing, and strengthening. As one fourteen-year-old student wrote about his experience with the Inner Strength System,

> *I didn't really like this class in the beginning because my grandmother had just passed away when it started, and I really didn't want to be here. I didn't want to be anywhere. But when I started coming to the class every week and started doing the thinking bubbles and the breathing I started to have fun. I started to just think about myself and think about doing things differently. The main reason why I didn't like this class that much was because you have to let go and forget, and I'm a person that keeps my guard up. I have to be strong because of lot of people died in my family and I have to be there for everyone else and do a lot at home. But long story short, I like this class. It opened me up a lot from how I used to be.*

Even among students who have suffered from trauma, as good educators and good mindfulness practitioners, we want to put into practice the art of not already knowing, not assuming that we are sure what a symptom or response might be without taking in the possibility of unexpected reactions. And always, exercise caution and seek professional or medical advice for the students without delay. We just never know all the details about the kids we work with or what might be presenting itself as an issue in one form or another. Teens don't always have the wherewithal or tenacity to insist when they may be being mis-read or mis-diagnosed; that's why we cultivate deep listening as part of our ability to see and feel into the situation before us. Anyone can fall prey to overconfidence, even those who have a lifelong practice of meditation.

> *In the summer of 1985 I travelled to Shelburne Falls, Massachusetts, to attend a ten-day silent mindfulness retreat taught*

by the late S. N. Goenka (1924–2013), a former businessman who began teaching a non-sectarian secular type of Vipassana or Insight contemplation in 1969. His courses reached over 100,000 people a year from settings as diverse as the private estates of the Indian elite to a maximum security Alabama prison. The film THE DHAMMA BROTHERS *documents the latter experiment. The structure around these retreats is intensive and simple. You are asked to observe the basics of your experience of breathing and sensations in your body in alternating sessions while you sit still in silence. This process of being in touch with the most elemental and universal aspects of our human experience, without props or dogma, stills the mind and allows deeper insight into the nature of human awareness to emerge. That also allows for aspects of our personal history and psychological makeup to become clear to us.*

I was feeling a little out of sorts when I arrived at the center. I thought it might just be the anticipation. I had just finished a 300-hour yoga intensive teacher-training course at a different center and was feeling stretched physically and mentally. I handed over my books and watch, ready to just be with the rudiments of my experience for ten days and was shown the way to my bunk in a dormitory-style tent. We were asked to be silent and to be respectful of the others who had also taken this time for contemplation. The next morning the first session began. I loved the stillness and sitting with others while sharing our common pursuit of insight into the nature of mind, and feeling, questioning our conclusions about reality. But by evening after the third day I began to feel more than uneasy. My body began to shiver, and I broke out into a heavy sweat all over my body. I went back to my bunk. I must have been whimpering. The next thing I knew an experienced retreat manager was standing over my bunk. She had heard that I was distracting the others with my shuffling and shaking.

"You're going to have to settle down and be more quiet," she said. "You are disturbing the others in the room."

"I think I have malaria," I said to her. Having already contracted the mosquito-borne infection in Delhi, India, the year before, I knew the signs.

"We see all kinds of symptoms arise when people sit still. All kinds of mental and emotional disturbances surface and show up in a variety of symptoms, sometimes even extreme ones. Things like what you are experiencing are not uncommon."

"I understand. I think I have malaria."

This conversation went back and forth for a while. I imagine I was less coherent than I remember, as the intense knocking feeling in my bones was reaching new intensity with its crescendo, and it seemed to be getting hotter and hotter in the tent.

In spite of her attempts to placate me, both my past experience and my experience of mindful observation made me pretty certain that there was something important that needed to be tended to. Medically.

"One of the other senior managers is also a doctor; he practices at the University of Massachusetts Medical Center, and I'll have him come and draw a blood sample for you." She still gave all indication that she expected this to turn out to be a tempest in a teacup.

I was moved into a quiet room in the main house. By the next afternoon, the results were back.

It was, in fact, malaria, the rarest of the four strains. I began the rounds of medication, which kill the parasites that multiply in the liver and release into the blood stream, attacking red blood cells and causing fevers of up to 105°F, shaking, and chills.

I remember just a little of the rest of the ten days. I used the practice as much as I could, and the experiment was intriguing. I saw a lot about mind-body connection and difference, and learned a lot about the movement of this illness. By the last couple of days, I was well enough to attend some of the talks, which emphasized observing, trusting your own experience, and being open to the unexpected. This retreat worked on the connection between the constant change in our physical experience, the change in the world, and the resilience and joy we develop when we can flow with that, and not grasp after any particular experience positive or negative.

In this case, the quiet confidence in my own experience that I had developed doing the practice enabled me to seek resolution even when the authority around me had doubts. It also enabled me to be firm without being combative or disrespectful of another's experience, even when that experience proved to be obstructive to what needed to happen. These are all twenty-first century skills we need to cultivate in our students, as well as in our adults.

I like to share this story with classroom educators and teachers of mindfulness. Although those circumstances of a retreat environment are different than an inner-city public school, many of the conditions are the same. Generally, in a classroom, we don't know who we are with or what their history is. And even if we do know their background, something unexpected may be occurring that we couldn't have anticipated. As the instructor said, mindful awareness is a powerful tool. It can help us discover inner stability. It can be a clear mirror reflecting our own bad habits, behaviors, and voice of conscience back to us. At times, it can stir up forgotten memories or traumas. It can trigger desires, happiness, fears, and hurts. I always remind my instructors to respect the delicacy of this work and be prepared to take signs of discomfort seriously and respond proactively. Sometimes it is best for students to sit through their discomfort and see how our minds manufacture difficulty for us. We often create our own dragons and scare ourselves with them. But not always. Sometimes it's best to call a doctor.

Tools for Teen Anxiety & Depression

Paying attention to the inhalation and exhalation generally has a soothing and quieting effect. It allows for integration between the input centers of our system. The body has three neurological centers: around the gut, the heart, and, of course, the brain. When we settle and synchronize these three, we feel more integrated, less pulled in different directions, more able to know who we are and what we feel. This gives us strength to think independently, to connect with others without fear of losing ourselves, and to be compassionate.

One student in one of my classes recently described how much anxiety she had in social situations, around tests, and when she gets into bed to sleep. Sometimes, she said, she stays up most of the night, too worried to close her eyes. The only time she ever feels at ease, she described, is rowing. She belongs to the city's only public crew team, and they practice hard on the city's beautiful Schuylkill River. When we began the quiet breathing exercises, she wasn't too sure. They brought up a little agitation, and I encouraged her to keep her eyes open and just be at ease.

One week the teacher brought the kids to a yoga space so they could be exposed to new places in the city and new wellness possibilities. I invited the kids to make themselves comfortable lying on mats and cushions while I guided them in a muscle-relaxation body scan. We had just talked about the way stress shows up in the brain and how the body needs rest for our cortisol levels to drop and for the body and mind to normalize again. The kids had learned about how to exercise the brain. We had talked about some of the intriguing neurological testing at the University of Wisconsin and how the FMRI scans showed that, when practiced, these mindfulness tools show drops in heightened anxiety responses in the brain. Zara was familiar with muscle awareness from her coach, and she settled into the exercise. I talked them through a series of exercises, tensing and relaxing the large muscles from the feet on up to their heads, encouraging them to let go and let gravity hold them. The room became restful and light. Some students dozed a little. Their teacher, on her own mat, looked ten years younger. Some minutes later I sounded the bell several times to end, and the teens began wiggling their fingers and toes, coming back into the world of engagement, out of their space of relaxation.

Zara looked up with a small smile lighting up her face. "I really let go," she shared, a little in awe of her own experience.

> *"It was like I was floating on the river, no nervousness. I even drifted off for a little while...that* NEVER *happens."*
>
> *She was so happy. Her face beamed ease. Her posture held a different confidence. Discovering that she could be relaxed in her own skin was going to be a game changer for her, and she felt it without needing to be told.*

Empowering youth with the means to cultivate ease and lightness of being gives them skills to last a lifetime rather than a set of answers that is useful for a single standardized test. Twelfth-century Jewish philosopher Maimonides[49] talked about the Eight Degrees of Charity, the highest being when we enable another to become self-supporting. When we teach another how to fish. Education is the gift we give our children. We don't often realize that our perspective is, in itself, an indicator and shaper of what is possible. Teaching them to see possibility is a gift that enables them to chart the future of the world.

Fishing Skills for the Twenty-First Century

Taking into account the infrastructure challenges and the meta-unknowns of technological advances and climate change, none of us can predict the future. We cannot see how our communications, economy, security, even food substances will change in the next few decades, within our own lifespan. So how do we educate for the future? The best preparation we can give is to prepare the students for that unknown, to teach them how to fish in uncertain seas.

The fishing skills for the twenty-first century[50] include flexible thinking, resilience, and an understanding of the momentum of influences over time. I would argue that twenty-first century skills also include being able to recognize the possibility of punctuated[51] change, of significant shifts that occur not on a linear schedule or growth trajectory. Backed by scientific evidence spanning millions of years and countless species, we see the possibility for significant shifts and evolution that we cannot foresee. These options excite an adolescent's imagination. It encourages their ability to peer into the future, their willingness to imagine and search, and their belief in the impossible. For all children, and particularly for students burdened by trauma, poverty, and a socio-economic structure that seems stacked against them, this outlook is not only congruent with evolutionary theory, it is also essential fuel for their perseverance.

The inability or unfamiliarity with seeing in context may be, in large part, responsible for short-sightedness, for political *ignorance* (ignorant meaning "not understanding"). It is the cause of much irresponsible, failed policy and poor macro decision-making. The remedy in education will be teaching children *how* to see, feel, and care, not just *what* we do about the immediate situations at hand. It becomes even more important for teens to learn about how to become aware because of the way the brain develops. During the period of the adolescent brain, roughly between the ages of 15 and 22 or on the outside between 12 and 30 years, the brain does not register long-term consequences emotionally in the same way that the adult brain does. That's why teens can reason the dangers of risky behaviors—like driving too fast, drinking too much, staying out too late on the wrong side of town—without *feeling* the potential consequences. And so they often do things that get them in trouble, in spite of themselves. When teens learn about the particular neurochemical changes in the teenage brain—for example, the changes in levels of dopamine—they have a better chance of building in safety precautions.[52] As one adolescent observed, "I know more about the brain and the way others may think or function in everyday life. I know how my peers may react to certain situations now, and I can learn to act accordingly." They take things less personally, seeing this is part of development and there are evolutionary reasons why the brain formed in this way.

We are influenced by all kinds of factors: our evolutionary roots, our cultural history, the makeup of our personal psyche, and so much more. In Eastern philosophy, there is a mythical metaphor called Indra's Net.[53] The net consists of an infinite number of intersections; at each corner glistens a multifaceted jewel that reflects and sparkles immeasurable reflections. Each jewel catches the reflections of other jewels and absorbs them into their own reflection, multiplying and re-communicating the images across the endless span of the universe. It is impossible to predict how the jewels and net will turn with any sway of the net. Everything is interconnected. One action has effects far beyond what can be seen. And so it is with each of our actions in the world. We cannot control our way into the future. There are too many unknowns. Too many delicate interconnections. But we can cultivate our skills to traverse the threads of the intricate net of consequence. That's when we realize how we educate the next generation means so very much about the world we are going to live in.

One of the students in the first Inner Strength classes I taught summed it up: "I learned how our actions affect others. And how we can have a good effect." This young man was quiet and studious. He took his meditation seriously when the rest of the class was resistant and disruptive. He studied martial arts and was used to the practice of being still. But the class was a tough one; it was one of those groups of kids that just hadn't jelled, making it that much harder for their teacher to teach. Cliques, disinterest, distractions.

The semester was a trial by fire. One of the classes was Halloween Friday. Try to get a group of unruly high school students dressed up as zombies with fake blood dripping down their faces to focus on their breath. Somehow, though, they did learn. This one student excelled. He asked subtle and deep questions about the brain, consciousness, connections with culture. About his own responses and cultural values. He was set on a track to a small, competitive, liberal arts college. He lived with his grandmother in one of the roughest parts of town, his parents long out of the picture. He worked as well as being civically engaged. He kept to himself for the most part, but the other kids liked him. Then summer came.

When I saw him the next semester, he looked completely different. He didn't notice me in the halls, didn't say hello. For a few weeks this went on, and I brought it up with the counselor and teacher. They both talked with him. It had been a rough time. He had come out as gay and had his affections rebuffed. He went into a tailspin. Quit martial arts. Became lackluster in his classes. His grades started to slip.

His cohort began their second round of mindfulness work. He began to re-engage. By the end of his senior year he had grown tremendously and was the recipient of a full scholarship to one of the best small liberal arts colleges in western Pennsylvania, on track to be a criminal justice attorney.

He spoke about what helped him through: "Seeing how each one of my actions affects everyone else. I could see it wasn't only about how I felt. I could see my actions could do good, that I could affect others in a positive way. Meditation helped me see the connections, and objectivity on thought helped me see that I didn't have to go with the first thing I felt. Then I put that together with culture, how it evolves, what I'm in the middle of, and how connected we are. Paying attention to all this helped me move past a very dark time in my life."

CHAPTER VI

The Quality of Our Relatedness

Trayvon we miss you
I hope you listening
This shit ridiculous
I had to mention it
But shame on you
I didn't wanna blame you
But they tried to frame me
And I get to aiming
The reason why I'm saying this cause
Black lives matter, black lives matter, black lives matter.

Dae Dae
"Black Lives Matter"

Inner, Inter & Meta Views

Whatever our future looks like, we will still have our own interiors, meaning we will always be in relationship with ourselves. We will still interact with others, with the world around us, and with all of the creatures and life that inhabit our biosphere. And we will still conform to some meta-views guiding our sense of right, wrong, and everything in-between.

Are we conscious of how we are shaping those meta-views? Who is helping us formulate what those guidelines are? Who is helping us refashion our values and ways of connectedness? Are we aware of an Indra's Web of interconnectedness and consequence, or do we still see the world as a confusing and overwhelming series of discreet occurrences and actors?

The skill to put events in context and to see the immeasurable effects and influence of events on life may in a large part determine how we will get through the tectonic upheavals of the coming period.

The three levels or dimensions of human relatedness—inner, inter, and meta—are distinct and intrinsically related. How we relate to ourselves (inner-personal) and how we relate to others (inter-personal) are the levels of relatedness and relationship we are most familiar with. I experience, I feel. I write and you read. She teaches, he learns. Our interaction, the process, experience, and interchange of relatedness itself is one that humanists, cyberneticists, and ecological or systems philosophers like Gregory

Bateson[54] intuited another way to interpret reality. Looking at our over-arching framework of beliefs or meta-views, we find them to be fixtures of convictions that we can lean into, explore, and even change. Recognizing our own capacity for choice over our perception and interpretation of reality is a powerful way to start opening up fixed, limited, and negatively defining self-assessments, prejudices against others, and pessimism about the future. In simple ways, this helps teens cope.

> *"The Inner Strength class even helped me outside of school. I remembered how to be more non-judgmental and accepting of feelings—I cannot control my feelings, but I can control how I respond to them."*

Let's unpack this a little. Teachers look at how well they teach, convey information, communicate. They even look at the effects on their students. Do students learn, grow, respond, succeed? This fourth component makes us look at: What is the quality of our interaction? What are we putting into the space between us? What hangs in the air? What atmosphere does it create? What residue does it leave? These questions point to the currency of relatedness. They value the process and exchange between us. They look at the current and residual effect of the process we set in motion as important in and of itself. This is significant because the currency of our relatedness transmits values beneath the surface of our interactions. And this sub-current of judgments affects how we perceive reality and what we believe is possible. The quality of our exchange can transmit the preference of kindness and generosity, or mistrust and violence. As one eighth-grade boy said,

> *I like to use the love and kindness meditations because it made me realize that I had a whole lot of people that deserve*

a lot of kindness. It made me pretty grateful and kinder. I also liked to imagine putting thoughts that were bothering me into bubbles and watching them float away. Not only did it calm me down, it made me smile a little.

We can fill the environment of our classroom with a quality of compassion and light heartedness, or fear and mistrust. The quality or currency of our relatedness creates social norms. Those norms affect us both consciously and unconsciously. Consider the quality of relatedness in Mother Theresa's Home for the Destitute & Dying (now called the Home of the Pure Heart) in Kolkata, India. In your corner coffee shop. In Nazi Germany. In the strip mall in your closest suburb. In the bodega in the ghetto. What is the different quality of interaction you perceive and experience or imagine in each of those places? What are the values being transmitted? What is the shared consciousness of each of these places?

Children are like sponges. They absorb more than they are consciously aware of. Becoming sensitive to the quality of interaction and the quality of the space between us means we can support the education we are imparting with the kind of curiosity, encouragement, and faith in the future that we want our students to feel. There are tools to engage with our experience at this level, and they are classroom appropriate. Mindfulness exercises are potent ones because of the quality of awareness they give us access to. Contextual or systemic thinking is a little more challenging, but with some well-designed guided stories or imaginative scenarios, children can grasp in a visceral way how there is a sense of awareness that is greater than the sum of each individual part.

When we are looking for an emergent property or possibility and we are teaching students how to see in context so they can grasp overarching meta-views and currents of change to allow for positive growth, one of the most essential things to see is the *quality* of relatedness that is occurring. What is the quality in the environment? In our interaction? In the room after we are still? By seeing these elements, kids can learn how to nourish and protect themselves. Just as bark protects the vulnerable tree trunk, we can protect ourselves from pollutants in our surroundings. While we are influenced by the meta context of events around us, we can minimize its toxicity to ourselves, and we can use that protectiveness in healthy and wholesome ways, not creating further residue of trauma.

Children from poverty are often exhorted to "rise above their circumstances," without knowing what that is supposed to mean. Usually it produces the attitude that one should wall off the violence or frightening experiences as if they didn't happen. Not surprisingly, this results in ongoing distortion and often uncontrolled, disruptive behavior. Though a lotus rises above the muck of the pond floor, its long stem and roots still trail in the mud, drawing nutrients that sustain it. Integrating, transcending, and transforming our outlook on life is different from disowning or trying to cut ourselves off from the process that led to our current existence.

Encouraging a child to leave behind everything about their roots, even from the poverty of the slums, can inadvertently sever their tender connection with their past, family, neighborhood—their sense of belonging. Just as the stolen generation in Australia were literally that, stolen from their environments and placed in foster care, leaving them orphaned and adrift, when we insist that kids rise up and out of their circumstances we invite disassociation from what made them who they are. In a world that is already so fragmented, wanting to disassociate kids from their home life, even for seemingly good reason, separates them from their roots, which means they cannot draw nutrients and wisdom from their own lives, from their own learned experience, from connection and love with their tribe, however imperfect.[55] We all gain strength from transmuting and transforming the dross of suffering into the gold of insight. We are embedded, interrelated with our circumstances, and with the inter-being that all of our interactions are continuously creating. What we can do is transform our *relationship* to the circumstances of our lives. We can transcend its limitations, trauma, and shadow. We can do this so completely that we grow into different people. We grow out of the limitations and shadow that those traumatic circumstances inflicted on us. We allow ourselves to shift tracks, shift courses. Then we find ourselves doing things that would have been antithetical to our previous selves. Antithetical to the protective measures we developed to cope. We don't need to remain a victim all our lives. But it takes something to grow out of the person that suffering shaped us into. We can stretch beyond what previously seemed impossible when we have space and insight that enables us to do so. That is part of the wonder of the human character and also of the resilience of our natural world. Working with adversity in this way, we bias positivity. We favor the goodness of life and seek strength and support amidst adversity, not merely outside of it.

There are many ways we grow up and out of our former selves. Cognitively and conceptually, we grow by understanding the complex circumstances that gave rise to the conditions we found ourselves in. We learn to depersonalize the circumstances. We grow by reaching towards possibility. Like plants that reach towards the sun, we are inspired by potential that captivates our attention and draws us towards it. The great French paleontologist Teilhard de Chardin (1881–1955) postulated what he called the "Omega

Point," a higher form of love and integration in the future, pulling the human family towards itself, while simultaneously validating the presence of that higher human capacity in the present. He intuited this as a medic in the bloody trenches of World War I. We can see from the midst of great suffering that we can grow. Transform. Become more integrated, whole, fulfilled individuals by shifting the context. And for the most part, we do that by learning to let go and look. When kids learn to do this, their outbursts settle down; their attitudes towards each other are tempered with more kindness, greater friendliness.

In the midst of challenge in the present, when we learn to anchor ourselves in a new story we begin to take hold of our lives in a powerful new way. We connect ourselves to a different story than the one our past laid out for us. We are pulled by and simultaneously pull towards a very different reality which becomes our own. In part by design and desire, and in part by not knowing and surrender, we let go and allow the current of our essential human goodness to take a new course. Supported by the right mentorship, small trim-tab adjustments, we gain our own confidence and our own feet. As adults, we do this more and more consciously, already mature enough to be architects of our own lives. For our children, we educate them to see this way, and we model this possibility. Students then mimic the educator's openness, their attitude towards others as one of understanding and potential. As this seventeen year old described:

> *My mindfulness instructor was a great teacher throughout the entirety of the mindfulness classes. I believe that her personality played a huge part in my understanding of each lesson. I am thankful for her teaching me the importance of understanding myself and my capabilities. Understanding myself includes*

> *knowing the things that I like and dislike, care for and aren't that interested in, and most importantly, understanding my personal coping techniques. We learned where those things come from. For example, how my preferences come from my background, my brain, and even how culture has changed. During this class one of the most important things I picked up on was realizing that what I feel is important, and being respectful as I perceive this awareness. For example, if I feel that when I am talking to someone that they are ignoring what I am saying, then I am going to be offended. In that moment, I would stop to express how I feel in a calm and assertive manner without being disrespectful. I learned how to see myself and see others at the same time. The thing that helped me the most was learning how to relax and maintain composure no matter the circumstance.*

Expanding our worldview to take in more long-term factors and influences zooms us out from the microscope under which we customarily look at influences and triggers. When we expand the context, we see more, we have more mobility, we have a higher vantage point. As we transcend the limitations of the circumstances we came from, we also create the conditions for emergent potentials. New possibilities, new ways of being together. Students may not be able to articulate what is happening within them with this complexity, but the results are moving and make their lives much happier.

Is the Past Also the Present?

When I was in Australia recently, I became absorbed by the landscape. Away from phones and for the most part Wi-Fi, I was conveniently removed from my customary habits and the draws for my attention. I was able to listen. Not listening to anything in particular or for anything in particular. Just listening. The longer I was there, the more I could sense, hear, feel. As if by listening, I could absorb the landscape into me. The bird calls, their whips, whistles, caws, and bells. The brush of wings. The rustle of dry gum leaves and paper bark. The thump of wallabies and little joeys beside them. Oh, and the cicadas with their endless music, and the butcher-birds and gerygones singing the melody and raga of the bush. Grounding it, maintaining it. It wasn't just sounds I was drawing into me; it was a merging with the lifeblood of the mountain, canyon, and dove-white coast.

There were artifacts, some 14,000 years old, in the hills where I was. The presence of the footsteps of these ancestors hung in the air. As I listened, it was as if I could hear them, too. Their remains part of the humus that softens sound in the wild, their presence still there, still coloring the landscape. My own steps and movements also now part of the symphony. The echoes of generations past *and* future all at once. In the dreamtime of the aboriginal people, past, present, and future are all merged into one. In some of the more far-out theoretical physics there is a theory of time collapsed into itself, or that it is a process that bends in a three-dimensional motion, more like a sphere or a torus, rather than a line,[56] in a single flow, pouring over and into itself. In some way, this type of seeing fits with our dominant paradigm. The past sets certain actions in motion, which create certain possible outcomes and eliminate other possible outcomes. Our present reality is influenced and to some extent determined by those outcomes. And our actions similarly shape the future. The past is very much alive in our present, and the future is also directly shaped by every single action now. Is there a way of seeing that takes all this into account viscerally? Not through reasoning or deduction, but through an apprehension, an awakening that illuminates to us a profoundly different sense of time?

Realizing there are other valid paradigms and ways to see the world softens the edges of what we take to be possible and allows new ways of seeing to emerge. We start to see that our worldview is constructed, agreed upon by the dominant culture, and that it is not the only way of seeing. The way we customarily perceive time, history, causality, or consciousness may not be the deepest, most inclusive way, or the way that gives rise to the highest human potentials.

I am not a romanticist for past worldviews. We cannot go back to an age before technology or literacy. But other cultures were privy to understandings that we cannot discern now. We have indeed forgotten some knowledge. While we can open up to those worldviews, I am not sure that we will be able to authentically intuit that knowledge in its fullness anymore. Times, and our sense of consciousness, have changed too much. But we can become sensitive to the possibility and to an intuitive knowing of life that is more inclusive and subtle than the framework we currently operate in. Our current worldview, as we've talked about, so bluntly separates me from you, present from past, self from other, human from world. That's the reality kids experience. There is another credible way to see the world.

In the period after World War I, Alfred North Whitehead moved from Britain to become dean of philosophy at Harvard, having never taught nor taken a philosophy class before then. It was at Harvard that he began to call a more inclusive and relational view "process" and proceeded to articulate a philosophical view of the world that became known as process philosophy. Rather than a series of discreet events, he saw everything as a flow, as experience. Gregory Bateson called this relatedness. Bateson would not see the five fingers on a hand; he would see how they related, the space between them. A worldview that does not harshly divide us in the way the Cartesian worldview does gives us access to very different resources. Individually, when we feel a part of something we experience safety, rest. Not so small or alienated as we so often feel in our vast and fast-paced world. Non-separate from the newborn, healthy or struggling for his first breaths, or the early humans just learning to spark fire from twigs and tinder, or the technologist plotting trajectories on graphs to program a flight path to Mars.

A process-oriented view has many dimensions and capacities, many ways of looking in. It is different from our own in these ways: First we see that our own worldview is constructed, a *set of beliefs* that orders reality. Then we see that it is not the only way to see reality. Then we allow ourselves to consider other paradigms and worldviews, and we allow ourselves to let go of our moorings and be informed by other possible ways of seeing the world around us. Once we consider alternative views, we open the door to creativity, expansion, solutions, and connections.

While it may sound destabilizing to consider alternative worldviews, those individuals who are most able to see the world from various vantage points are able to leave room for new possibilities, for open gates around the corner of what seems like a brick wall. They can intuit punctuated change that has the capacity to avert a linear course of destruction.

Kids find adventures in paradigm shifts thrilling. They love the possibilities and find the exploration wild and risky—in a safe way. A teen's desire to explore and push the boundaries becomes a creative imagining of how the world can be, resulting in new inventions, new sounds and music, new dress, new language. Exercises in paradigm shifts allow them to question authority, and what would teens rather do than that?

What Is a Paradigm Shift

Right now, students for the most part, are unconsciously being taught—and are adopting—the Cartesian worldview. This view sees "us" and "them," humans and the rest of the world, mind as separate from body/matter/form. Based on the profound and, at the time, radical insights of René Descartes, this shift in paradigm and worldview, in how we see and relate to everything else revolutionized thinking. Now we can see that way of interpreting how the world works is one way, a single way. A method and view that replaced earlier thinking, and one that can be replaced should we find a worldview that transcends this way of thinking. One that offers a more subtle, more complex, more elastic, and more useful lens through which to view the world around us. It is important as educators—or as students—first to recognize that we have adopted a worldview. And that has been from the choices presented to us, and they influence the way we assimilate fundamental ideas and beliefs from the world around us. When we recognize that we are seeing the world one particular way, and can see the world differently, this has a profound effect on our ability to assimilate new ideas, new ways of being in the world. Seeing the worldview we currently use, even without being able to replace them with more inclusive ones, is a large part of seeing in context.[57]

All the great philosophers and social revolutionaries have been able to question the worldview they were submerged in and intuit new possibilities for ordering and structuring reality. Nelson Mandela was able to see a world of white and black equality in apartheid South Africa. Mother Theresa was able to see worth and dignity in the throwaway lives of the dying poor in Calcutta. Galileo was able to see the Earth revolving around the Sun and the social implications of that shift in perspective. Twentieth-century philosopher, linguist, and mapmaker of the structures of human consciousness Jean Gebser[58] (1905–1973) saw emergent capacities of consciousness, positing a different relationship to time, space, and presence. Contemporary scientists like David Christian[59] see the world in Deep Time, as a single continuum from the origin of the universe some 13.7 billion years ago. Paleontologist Teilhard de Chardin saw the world in a state of perpetual evolution, reaching towards higher coherence and forms of Love. Newton saw the world with static pieces interacting with each other while Einstein saw relative or related reality influencing the outcomes of what occurs.

How do we get children to begin to question the paradigm they are assuming without creating instability? How do we get them to begin to see the world in new ways that have the power to create a whole new layer of stability in an environment that is constantly in flux? This is the kind of questioning and education that will prepare them for the future. It's the kind of education that requires partnership with the teachers on a journey of mutual discovery. It requires authority and mentorship from the teachers without the force and control that chafes at teens and causes them to rebel.

And, as a note to all educators, while the Inner Strength System is being used with students from all types of backgrounds, contemplative work and applied philosophy is not for every student. Conscious educators also need to be sensitive to anxiety that can arise when students are uncomfortable with this type of challenging inquiry and be ready to respond quickly and appropriately.[60] We want to model flexibility authentically, by not being attached to a specific mode or way of learning. Then we'll be free to respond and support, and students will be free to heal and learn.

CHAPTER VII

Looking Out from the Center

Sky of blackness and sorrow
Sky of love, sky of tears
Sky of glory and sadness
Sky of mercy, sky of fear
Sky of memory and shadow
Your burning wind fills my arms tonight
Come on up for the rising
Come on up, lay your hands in mine
Come on up for the rising
Come on up for the rising tonight.

Bruce Springsteen
"The Rising"

The Center Point of the Circle | Globalization & Connection

Part of the way we begin to understand worldviews is we look for the center point of the circle we inhabit. What is the vantage point from which we peer out into the vast world around us? For most individuals who have embraced the interconnectedness of a globalized culture, that vantage point is all of humanity. We see, feel, and care about the totality of the human beings on the planet, knowing that for all the differences between us, we are one single family. Many individuals who begin to intuit this type of interconnectedness also begin to identify the shared nature of everything on this single planet. What Apollo astronaut Edgar Mitchell so movingly spoke about after he saw our tiny blue orb floating in space was his desire to take all human beings up above the Earth's atmosphere. He felt that once we were able to see, with our own eyes, the beautiful single sphere we all inhabit, it would change our reference point on life fundamentally.[61] When our vantage point shifts in this way, the single globe serves as the center point of our frame of reference. When we look from here, we find our safety in our interconnectedness with all inhabitants, with all breathers of the same air, all fish, fauna, and fowl, and the plants, insects, buildings, machinery, knowledge, and technology. Everything. At a visceral level, we appreciate that our fates are intertwined, that care for another on the other side of the world in crisis, in hunger, in poverty, in fear, is care for our own self, our own fate. Raising the level of conversation towards deeper communion brings compassion for all those around us. It brings about both greater sensitivity for the universal and the personal. Personal love requires a great deal from the individual, an ability to forgive and accept, to connect across differences, to recognize common denominators when language, ethnic background, political beliefs are at odds. This is challenging. Kids may have a better chance if we give them reason to look at the world this way.

Not all people share this global view. A protectionist worldview is far more common, and increasingly so. Of late, defending a nationalist worldview has resurfaced in its popularity. It is seen as a refuge from the rising waters of global challenges. When nationalists look out to the world, the ground they stand on is defined by their own nation-state. Those drawn borders of a single flag limit their connectedness—and to some extent, their care. "My nation first" is that cry. That sense of belonging is to specific borders, and that belonging can spawn a degree of loyalty and allegiance that enables powerful focus and commitment within a set sense of parameters. The adherence to this worldview creates larger protection around a home, a neighborhood, a city. It creates strength through identification with a larger group, in protection of itself, defining its uniqueness in relation to and as other than the masses. It relies on a dichotomy, an us-them, for identity and can provide a clear and compelling sense of being met in one's needs. Sacrifice is for those who resemble oneself. There is a sense of nobility in that sacrifice and in the recognition of that sacrifice and loyalty by others who are both same and different.

We tend to feel more comfortable with those like us. Those who share our beliefs and history. Those who share our myths, origin stories, values. Those with whom we can converse deeply, further our understanding without having to start at the beginning all over again. These boundaries can stretch wider than a tribe and smaller than the globe. All Christendom can include individuals who speak Swahili and Italian. At times, it can spread across nations but not across the street. The nationalist view is being fanned these days as people fear a loss of safety and plenty. But there are other ways to understand the world that will lead to greater security, greater plenty. To get there, we have to pass through a level of discomfort and unfamiliarity first. Creating conscious classrooms that educate for the future depend on this.

A developmental worldview recognizes the concentric or nested nature of our identifications.[62] It recognizes the value of each view, and the distinctions. As one awakens to each more inclusive worldview, one loses some of the advantages and sensitivities of the others. A profoundly open worldview allows for the movement between different vantage points depending on the situation, recognizing the rights, needs, and legitimacy of different worldviews,[63] and fostering a powerfully unitive embrace of the distinctions.

> *At the end of the semester I subbed for one of my instructors, who is a retired firefighter. He travelled ten hours every few weeks just to teach mindfulness and a developmental perspective to high school students. He is a quiet man, reserved and understated, a deep practitioner who loves to meditate, and someone with a wealth of stories that get the kids' attention. Firefighters have first-hand experience of consequences of teen impulsivity and risk-taking. His descriptions of tending to teens who bungee jumped from a bridge into a too-shallow river, delivering a baby at the side of the road, or pulling a knife out of a wounded individual create a lot of street cred.*

And when he credits meditation for helping him keep his cool and better assess the situation, they listen.

When I met with his students, I shared with them why he leaves his home and stays in Philadelphia just to teach them.

"My vision is to reach a significant percentage of high school kids in Philly with mindfulness and this developmental perspective. Dave is so committed to that he drives all the way here, stays a few weeks, then heads home for a few days, just to turn around and come back. Dave spent thirty years with the fire department. He's seen more dangerous situations than any of us can imagine, and he's seen how much people can help each other and work together. He understands what really brings human beings together. Imagine in ten years if every student in the city learned the art and science of mindful relationships? What would this city be like? What would our firefighters and city council-persons be thinking then? What would high school teachers be like? How would the police officers and engineers and city planners and chefs and medical assistants and everyone else be relating to their jobs, their potentials, and each other? When we can change our worldview by being still, making space, and questioning the paradigm we use to see the world, we change culture."

The room, which was filled with some of the more distracted and disinterested students, got still.

"You mean, you want to do this for ten years with kids like us?" one young man asked.

"That's right," I nodded.

There was a spontaneous exclamation. The penny, it seemed, had dropped.

The kids experienced how we believed in them and in what we were doing. More importantly, they saw that what they were doing was a culture hack. They could be part of a positive disruptor just by watching their breath, creating space, and connecting the dots.

"Who wants to lead the closing meditation?"

A rough and socially awkward kid jumped to the front. The principal credits this program for this young man's high school graduation. Without the self-regulation he learned, he would almost certainly have been expelled even though he is bright and does like to learn.

"Listen up, you all. Sit up. Quiet. No phones." Cla-a-a-ang, he sounded the bell.

He guided us through his own version of a space-making meditation. "Be quiet. Feel the space. Let your problems go." Then he ended, "Send good vibes to everyone you know, and don't forget yourself. Tell yourself you can do it."

With students, if we only give import to the report-card *A* or the science trophy, or the lead in the school musical rather than the extension of emotional support to a fellow student whose dog just died, or encouragement to a friend stricken with stage fright, or to maintaining calm in the face of bullying or rivalry, then the acts which are motivated by values of the experience of unity, kindness, generosity of spirit, and belief in another's ability to do well are by default devalued. We see this bias towards accomplishment rather than towards the experience of interconnectedness all around us.

When we relegate positive social connections, compassion, and happiness as unimportant, unseen, they are deemed expendable. And when they are determined to be expendable, we discourage the striving, strength building, and risk taking that it takes to truly live in accordance with those more gracious human expressions and higher human values. When we discount those qualities externally and internally, our children fail to practice them. And when they don't learn how to practice connection, kindness, and sensitivity, they find themselves adrift, alienated, and unable to minister to themselves or others. No wonder our children feel alone, disempowered, and angry.

Teaching students to set positive ripples in motion, without needing to be identified as the rock that falls into the pond, reduces the negative poles of addiction to the limelight or fear of being seen. When students become more aware of how we all contribute to *all* of our experience, they learn to become sensitive to the flow of life and to the quality of their experience. They learn to find their agency and accomplishment in relationship to their effect on the whole. Focusing on the positive effect they can have on their own experience and the experience of others gives them a greater sense of purpose and connection.

School Climate | Group Consciousness

Classroom climate, meaning the behavior and respect in a school, is an issue in contemporary urban classrooms. Usually, climate refers to toxic culture, violent culture, or distracted culture. School psychologists and intervention specialists see the culture primarily as the sum total of the individual actions, and they try to mitigate the negative influences. In order to improve the culture, those professionals endeavor to change the individual and to compel him or her towards different behaviors. That doesn't work very well, and it is incredibly labor intensive. Each intervention ends up being personalized and specific. While that may also be needed, the group doesn't benefit from others' instruction, and so the interventions don't really have a cumulative nature on the group as a whole.

What if we looked at this differently? Let's look at classroom culture primarily as the consciousness that is the backdrop or presence of the classroom. Class culture is like partially blended flavors of a complicated soup stock. Flavors that have been stewed together over different lengths of time, leading to layers and layers of subtlety and currents that make themselves apparent depending on what other ingredients they interact with. Like herbs in a soup, every individual and every intervention contributes to the climate, but what will tweak the collective consciousness and shift it from hostile to nurturing may not be the obvious. And if you've ever over flavored a soup with a bit too much tarragon, you know what I mean. When kids start to intuit that the climate they experience is something they are *all* creating, it pulls out the better part of them. Kids are sensitive. With pointers, they can experience how they can have distracted minds and that it doesn't need to change to positively affect the whole. They can experience that their effort to be mindful, their practice of being focused—even if they still feel distracted, agitated, or sad—has a positive effect on the whole. They don't need to get rid of their troubles. Their focus and effort to be aware and nonjudgmental of themselves brings a sense of well-being and support into the space between everyone. They can improve class climate with shared commitment.

That's why when it comes to shifting the culture of a school or a class, I recommend that we support necessary personal interventions with training that works with all students together. We can, at times, more easily shift the feeling between us than the problems of any particular individual. We all are affected by the status quo. Our personalities distort when that status quo is critical, negative, or unsafe. If the prevailing status quo is unwholesome, our affect and the way we present ourselves will be contorted according to our particular reaction to that context. When we bring the tools of mindful awareness into the classroom and begin by setting all of our focus in a contemplative or empathetic direction, it warms the climate. Working with those tools consistently over time has a long-lasting effect. It has a positive and cumulative effect unlike disruptive disciplinary measures against an individual. If we shift the focus from the individual to the qualities that we want to arise from the collective of students, we shift the primary object of our awareness to something everyone can participate in, together. The shared values and will of the class then becomes the shaper and protector of the shared space. Then we can look at how motivation, intent, contribution, awareness, respect, and openness all contribute positively to the overall climate in the room.

Students like to become aware of currents and qualities. The shy smiles I see steal over unguarded faces when they experience that sense of quiet and well-being are priceless. They learn not to personalize their reactions automatically, which helps them choose different responses even to taunts or disappointments. One fourteen-year-old proudly told me that when her boyfriend broke up with her she wanted to say all kinds of things to him, but she went upstairs to her room, calmed herself down with some mindful breathing, and then just let it go. She smiled, "I couldn't change what he said or how I felt, but I didn't have to say what I wanted to say to him." Her victory changed her ability to be present in class. All of a sudden, it felt like she landed. She arrived and carried herself like she belonged. Once she took her place in the class, she was able to be taught, and she also started encouraging others to participate. When something works, kids can't help but want to share it with their peers.

When students start looking at the space between us and how we interact with that space, they stop trying to take responsibility for something they cannot control. Yet they become sensitive, awake and aware, able to rebalance. They start valuing their own calm in a disturbed environment. They start being able to pursue their own motivation in a dull environment. It is moving and powerful when students start working together to shift the quality of the environment. They metaphorically link arm in arm, connecting to each other, sensitive to the quality of the class climate or the group consciousness. When that happens, I step back and let them make choices to support each other. One student can shift the attitude of a struggling individual or a stubborn clique, and that changes the overall personality of a disgruntled class.

One day I arrived in one of my favorite classes. I knew the students and teacher well, and their cohort was always amiable and respectful. As usual, we began with focusing on the sound of a chime and then practiced mindful breathing for five or ten minutes. I asked them what they experienced, what was the quality in the room? To me, it felt unusually disturbed and distracted in an unpleasant way. Several of the kids said they felt kind of out of sorts, for no particular reason. They felt agitated and restless, but as far as they could tell it was just an ordinary day, nothing particular to cause anxiety or stress. No big exams, papers, reviews. We talked about how sometimes there are things happening beyond our control that have noth-

ing to do with us. At those times, rather than looking for a cause in ourselves, something specific we are worried about or that we did wrong or have forgotten to do, it's best to go about our day, taking care to be particularly kind and considerate so we don't spill our unidentified nervousness onto the people around us or into the shared space. We went on with the lesson, never quite lifting that sense of something out of place, but also not further confusing ourselves by mis-identifying the causes as something any of us personally did wrong.

After class I touched base with the school counselor. Before I described the class's experience, she shared with me that earlier that morning school security had taken a student out of class in handcuffs. This happened in the room two doors down from where I was teaching. The youth was usually a quiet young man. He had blown up at a teacher, and his age, size, and degree of frustration posed enough of a concern that they had to remove him from the school. The teacher was known among students and staff to be a bully. She had been unfairly pressuring and reprimanding this student, pushing him to the breaking point. Provoked, he verbally snapped, an event that, given his race and socio-economic class, could prove to be a life-determining incident. I don't know what happened in this case, though I know the principal was aware of the complexity and would have gone to great lengths to de-escalate the issue for everyone's sake.

The counselor let me know that word hadn't spread throughout the school yet. My students, who had been so agitated, would have had no idea. Hearing the story confirmed what we all seemed to feel in the collective atmosphere. Helping the students be at ease with not knowing why they felt dis-

quiet without drawing negative conclusions about themselves meant that when they did hear the story, they would realize first how interconnected we all are, second how the class climate reflected the disturbance and anguish of the student and the aggression of the teacher, and third that even though they felt disturbed, they had done nothing wrong. The students were beginning to become aware that we feel the impact of the activity around us, and it takes inner strength to stay on course when the environment is pulling us off track. The teens also began to be aware of the way their own steadiness and positive contribution to the shared space makes a difference for everyone.

There aren't hard borders or boundaries that can completely eliminate influences on us. Our awareness is permeable. With deep, contemplative focus we can lessen the negative imprints we experience from harshness in the world around us. This helps us filter the incoming in a constructive way. Like a horse pulling a tourist buggy in the city wears blinkers to shield him from startling traffic, we want to teach kids how to intelligently and effectively be able to protect themselves from external influences that are distracting, disturbing, or depleting.

Decades or centuries from now, we may look back on this time and realize that the pressures on our delicate ecosystem, the pollutants, overcrowding, factory farming, contaminated waterways, and species degradation are a large contributor to the undefined anxiety that so many of us experience, a level of anxiety that has been on the rise the last thirty years or so.[64] Even if we don't consciously register these pressures, we don't exist in isolation. The pressures on the very earth we stand on, and on our co-inhabitants, affect us and communicate a distress we are registering but not quite sure what to attribute it to. This is also good news. Delight, hopefulness, support, and environmental re-generation equally affect our consciousness. And the upliftment of even small moments of joy and small glimpses of beauty have a power of their own. What I've seen is that one teacher's encouragement, optimism, and faith in her students can draw a class to reach for success. The immediate, positive connection registers in a child's system louder than an amorphous negative in the general environment. Contact and relationship make all the difference.

Part of shifting classroom culture is focusing on openings, breakthroughs, small successes. This allows for improvement in the overall culture for everyone. It enables everyone to experience upliftment. While mindfulness practice guides us to be with what is, it also supports us to connect with the joy of life, that lightness of being that we feel in small moments that touch us without cause. As teachers, drawing attention to openings, positive shifts, creativity, beauty in a school environment, and pointing out these uplifting experiences makes them real for students. Making that link between these eruptions of joy and the higher aspects of our human potential puts students' attention on the positive. They see tangible signs that belie the hype or division that sells more news. Educating children to bias the wholesome, to give it attention, and nurture it trains them in important ways. What we put our attention on will influence how we feel and what we believe is possible.

Schools are unusual environments, and we can create meaningful and focused containers for contemplation within those four classroom walls. Each school has its own culture, its own codes, visible and hidden. I have seen phenomenal changes in high schools when the principal has valued the insight that contemplative practices bring. Without disrupting the academic flow, a school can incorporate training and space for quiet compassion towards oneself and others, inquiry into the nature of thought, and space for grief, loss, and healing. We can weave into our curriculum generative exercises that turn stress into fun, that identify success and setbacks for what they are, and teach students to look for their own glimpses of newfound inner strength. When one of the administrators I work with fundraised and turned a cluttered sports supply room into a sanctuary space for quiet reflection, it established value for the inner dimension among both students and faculty. Amidst college admissions posters, sports trophies, and health tips, there is now a tangible marker for those activities that look within for strength, happiness, and accomplishment. That's a new source of school pride.

Are We Solid or Flow? Wave or Sea?

The nature of light troubled scientists for centuries. The idea that something could be both tangible and wavelike, material and energetic at the same time was hard to reconcile. It had to be one or the other, so scientists thought. Generally, we bias the concrete or material and describe the flow as a quality of that object. But light seemed to also be "flow" without the "solid." This phenomenon of the universe has significant effects on how we can see and perceive the world and others around us.

We generally see unique individuals. We don't see "energy" or "consciousness" that arises out of a group of individuals. We see actions taken by individuals. But we could see currents in the sphere of interrelatedness being felt and interpreted by the consciousness of the individuals present.

Behind this contemplation is the question, are we the particle or the undulating current? Are we a separate wave or the single sea? Are we in some way both? As we allow ourselves to see ourselves as the actors and the acted upon, we can see that we are inseparable from our environment. We are not just solids unaffected by the flow all around us. Not just alien rocks from outer space plopped out of nowhere onto earth. We are all being acted upon, and that makes us part of the entire whole we arise from, inseparable from the process of emergence and dissipation. The recognition that we are part of a whole, inseparable from it, as a fundamental reference point for teachers and kids, changes the atmosphere of the classroom. It creates cohesion between students and instructors; it enables a natural care for others to arise since we all benefit when the whole does well. It reduces teen angst and negative self-focus, and it creates positives out of teen bonding.

Just as a wave arising out of the waters of the vast sea has its own shape and characteristics, so do we as individuals. The wave is, in many fundamental ways, indistinguishable from the whole it emerges out of. It also has its own unique characteristics; ask any surfer or kite-boarder or sailor. When we are looking out at our classroom of students, in some ways we see more unique ripples on the ocean's surface, each student and their life's trajectory or like an impulse that travels. They move, propelled by the influences on them. They operate in some type of vast continuum. Though they can hardly imagine it, that continuum began at the birth of the cosmos or before (with all the factors that gave rise to life-sustaining conditions) and will continue long after their mortal form has aged and lost its life force and the physical has returned to the elements from which it came.

Seeing out from this centerless center of process changes a teen's perspective on life and their ability to respond. Human beings are under an illusion of solidity. We build skyscrapers to last forever, yet the very substances that make up these monoliths are themselves in flux. We see ourselves as solid in a world of flow, like an actor in front of a green screen, but in reality, we are part and parcel of that process, inseparable from it. Our identity is intrinsic with the wave of life. Think about it, can we really separate ourselves—beings with consciousness—from the oxygen and hydrogen we take in? Where does life begin as distinct from lifeless elements? Where does sentience begin on the vast 13.7-billion-year continuum?

The value of a process-oriented perspective is that it recognizes that our experience is moving. We can see ourselves as wave and sea, without those two being mutually exclusive. We see that we emerge and differentiate and dissolve and absorb depending on what is most important at the time—whether it is the vast sea of humanity when we are looking at humankind's capabilities or our individual feelings when we are overcome with joy.

I use the words *flow* and *interconnectedness* interchangeably for a reason. I believe that as we see the degree of process, we will also see the degree we are co-joined. We can sense, without complicated or expensive experiments, that interconnectedness and movement are so intertwined they blend into one event. Teaching students to be able to perceive the world around them as process and as co-dependent is a powerful and insightful orientation. Rather than taking away their solid foundation, it gives them an intimate relatedness to each other and to the entire cosmos. It gives them a framework that can accommodate enormous change. It gives them a perspective that, in an increasingly alienating world, makes them feel and realize that they are not foreign or alien or expendable. It illuminates a relatedness that makes their individuality and humanity an extraordinary question mark, for out of this whole cosmos and all its possibilities how did they become the individual they are? And in the midst of this wonder and inexplicability of their own uniqueness, it also shows at an essential level they are also not so different from everyone else, not so foreign, and not so separate from all that is. This deep-time history of their origins gives teens a practical way to re-interpret challenging issues, find confidence and self-respect, and also ways to navigate what they cannot control by will power alone.

Students in inner city schools are generally taught information, rather than how to put all the pieces together in new ways. In one school that draws from the rougher zip codes in the city, I was sharing with students the developmental reasons why they do some of the things they get in so much trouble for.

"Think about it. In our cave-person past, once we reached fifteen or sixteen, our parents' generation only had a few more years to live. Life expectancy was roughly forty years, give or take, much shorter than it is now.[65] *When we hit our adolescence, we needed to gain all the skills necessary to survive in the clan. Our brains tricked us to take risks. What is the chemical that makes us feel excited?"*

"Dopamine!" a few kids shouted out. "That's the happiness drug!"

"What raises our levels of dopamine?"

"Fun stuff. Driving fast. Staying out."

"You think you like to do those things because you like them. But a long, long time ago your brain chemistry developed a way to trick you to want to do things that are risky so you would learn the skills you will need to live in the wild without your parents' generation to help you. You think you'd want to fight a saber-toothed tiger on your own without a nudge from your biology?

"You see, you're not always just making decisions. Very cleverly, your dopamine levels are extra low in the period of the adolescent brain. To get them to a level where you'll feel OK, you need some excitation. You're being tricked by your physiology to seek risk, danger, edgy things in order to feel OK." They looked amazed. Scientific proof that the shadow of our early ancestral past was manipulating them on Saturday night. Some relief crossed their faces. They weren't just stupid, rebellious, proud. They weren't just disobeying their mothers. They looked a little pumped, too, justified. They were, in some way, right.

"How much are you really making your own decisions, and how much are you like marionettes, being tugged on a string by your physiology?"

Hmmmm. They didn't like that so much. "Whether you have a quiet personality or a boisterous one, your brain chemistry is still pushing you to innovate, create, discover for yourself."

Some of the more quiet kids stopped shuffling in their chairs. They were included in this too.

"This phenomenon has been studied for a long time. And it has been tapped into by marketers all over the world. Think about it. How much are you being led by the gaming companies and

the soda companies to play more video games and drink more energy drinks so they can increase their profits? Next time you feel compelled to do something you know isn't good for you in the short or long run, think about how you might be being manipulated, and then think again for yourself."

I like to throw those examples in. Research shows that the most effective anti-teen-smoking campaigns put out by health departments were the ones that showed how the tobacco industry was creating advertising that relied on a teen's reduced ability to see long-term negative outcomes. When the health departments framed their anti-smoking message as "Don't be fooled" by the tobacco companies, "Don't get tricked into giving them profits for the next four, five decades," teens listened. Teens like few things less than being duped or used. Their rebellion was directed against the tobacco companies; it was a rebellion that wouldn't smoke as a statement of independence and cool.

"How much can we separate ourselves from everything going on around us? From all of the knowledge and all of the media influence? Now let's take that back a little further. How much can you separate yourself from the food you eat? When did that piece of pizza stop being pizza and become you? When did that starburst and all of the oxygen and hydrogen it released stop being some stuff way far away and become the air you breathed and the fuel that makes you run? When and where do you begin and end?"

"Whoa, that's deep," one kid said. Most of the students looked a little stunned. Their faces a combination of looks that were at once blank, confused, and a little curious.

"That's like when I get mad it comes back at me," one girl said.

"Explain."

"I used to think that was just like a saying. You know, what goes around comes around. But if we are all in this same place, and everything is pushing on all of us, then getting all up at someone else is getting all up in one space, and that's me too. It doesn't just come around. I'm in the middle of it!"

At that moment, in a very practical, down-to-earth way, the developmental or process-oriented perspective started dawning on her. Her face softened with a sheen of innocence, the happiness of discovery, of connection, of self-reliance. These are the moments that can make all the difference in an adolescent's life, insights that no one can take away because they have to do with a child's own discovery.

This interconnected perspective, with all its science and mystery, I believe is in large part how we're going to prepare the next generation sufficiently to intuit and innovate a better future. This is how we are going to strengthen them and wizen them to withstand the fracturing times we are experiencing and to paddle through the narrow chute in the rapids to clear water ahead. This is how we are going to free them from the divisive views of the past and the chains of fixed ideas so all of their teen creative freedom, risk-taking, and vision can skywalk the horizons of the present and peer into the future.

This perspective, with all its inherent intrigue and inquisitiveness, introduces teens to the great mission of our time in culture, while providing them with support and mentorship so they do not shoulder too much of a burden that isn't rightfully theirs. Theirs is one—but only one—chapter of this epic we call time.

Looking out in a classroom with this view gives me great optimism. It sheds light on the noble and hopeful project of designing new structures of culture that we can work on together in the present. It is how we can understand the notion of "the eternal present," for this perspective holds every drop and reflection of the past and contains within it infinite echoes of the generations yet to come.

CHAPTER VIII

Culture & Us

Now I've been crazy couldn't you tell
I threw stones at the stars, but the whole sky fell
Now I'm covered up in straw, belly up on the table
Well sang and drank and passed in the stable.

That tall grass grows high and brown,
Well I dragged you straight in the muddy ground
and you sent me back to where I roam
Well, I cursed and I cried, but now I know....

Ring like crazy, ring like hell
Turn me back into that wild haired gale
Ring like silver, ring like gold
Turn these diamonds straight back into coal.

Gregory Alan Isakov
"Stable Song"

From the First Peoples to the Next Peoples

When I first heard about Gaia or the earth as a living, breathing being, I thought it was a "new age" transference of human qualities onto something as vast as the universe. When I was a teenager, I wasn't into purple scarves, crystals, or anything that represented an airy, ungrounded, trivialization of the gravity of the task of being human on earth. Being a teen, my opinions were hardly nuanced, and like most teens, I thought that anyone who opened their eyes would surely see as I did. Fortunately, like most adolescents, I grew out of that stage. I was also a product of the seventies. Been there, done that. No longer starry-eyed angels of the sixties, believing in peace, love, and revolution. My generation thought that everything good had already been tried and had failed. It was hard for me to see experiments with new paradigms from fresh, uncynical eyes. The quote I put under my picture in my high school yearbook was from a song by the band The Who. It sardonically read, "There's no easy way to be free." But I was also an idealist and a seeker. I was looking for wisdom, just not sure if all the usual places—schools, relationships, religions, pop culture, or even the institutions of justice—could get me there. Fortunately, my cynicism was as much a fashion of the times as my flannel shirts and torn jeans, and my own curiosity about the meaning of life and what my actual purpose on earth was were the deeper currents of identity that drove me forward. And so I kept looking, reading, travelling, seeking, and questioning.

While the eighties did see a plethora of shamanism-lite, that decade also saw the first forays into the cultural mainstream of the tenets of a worldview that had been summarily overridden and cast aside by the marching boots of colonialism and industrialism. The New Age's early attempts to reach back into time and across cultural divides sought ways to connect that some intuited but didn't have sufficient wisdom or mentorship to discover. Over time, the translation of these ancient philosophies began to merge with contemporary sensitivities. Innovators began to create philosophical Venn diagrams between how our physiology works and what makes it thrive, and the wisdom that pre-modern imagery points to. This East-meets-West or Indigenous-meets-Quantum Physics made alternative ways of understanding reality more culturally acceptable.

Perhaps it was those bridges that also helped me be willing to venture into nature-mythic understandings of the world. These views feel the breathing, living cosmos and recognize our place in it as the micro-specs we are. They also respect and revere the life-force in each micro-spec, so we are both humbled and exalted, creators and in flow along with the vastness around us. We are interconnected in a way that is inseparable, a node in Indra's Net that contains, through reflection, the infinite faces of the whole. This sensitivity to wholeness as well as uniqueness becomes more urgent if we are not to lose 40,000[66] years of a way of life that formed images and languages out of the processes that tossed the swirling matter, light, and energy of our cosmos into the life-filled earth we inhabit. The better future we can build, I believe, will best emerge out of balance of these ancient-contemporary, mythic-rational polarities. It's a model that calls us to internalize the ethos of the First Peoples, where our wants are kept in moderation by our awareness of the tenuous balance of the whole. When we as a human species begin again to feel the imbalance of our bodies and the pressures on our earth, and we learn how to respond to those sensitivities in big and small ways, that would herald a very different relationship to the rest of life.

We currently have an educational reward structure that relies on standardized tests for bits of memorized information rather than on creative responses that show an integral or systemic understanding. If we are serious about the fact that we are educating the next generation of stewards of our world, then we will want to empower them with the greatest sense of the possible that we can. Change will still come slowly, but new potentials are more likely to emerge when we train our children to give credence to their own sense of the systemic fluidity of reality and the inherent potential that gives rise to.

Why is this so important? As anthropologists and urban planners assert, we live in a new era called the Anthropocene Age, where the actions of humans are determining the future of life on earth to a degree that has never happened before in the history of the planet. We can't go back. We can't unlearn or un-advance the advancements we've made. So we need to ensure we are as well-informed as possible in a world that is increasingly complex. To be that well-informed, we can't depend on information alone. We'd be overloaded and overwhelmed, even more than we are now. Through contemplative practice, we can build our capacities for observation, awareness, and sensitivity. Those capacities can help bring us the knowledge to be responsible in this new human-centric age.

The reason why this is so significant is that we have, for all intents and purposes, crossed a point where the future we inhabit will arise out of the changes human beings are already unintentionally setting in motion. These include but aren't limited to climate change, resource allocation, urbanization, habitat depletion, toxic waste, and increasing digitization. New opportunities will arise out of these conditions, no doubt. They do not automatically herald the end of humanity or of life, as we know it, in spite of both valid and sensationalized scripts. That is too simplistic and too reactive a conclusion to reach. But to fashion the trends that define an Anthropocene Age into a better future requires of us a heightened level of sensitivity, awareness, and creativity. We can educate for that; we can cultivate those skills in the next generation. But it takes something other than what we are currently educating towards.

Through the art of being still and being able to see what is, we cultivate the ability to make friends with what is troubling. We learn to value curiosity, and interest brings joy or at least lightness of being. Mindfulness has the mysterious capacity to bring about ease and a sense of well-being without needing to have sophisticated, interpretive frameworks around it. A teen will say, "I always got into a blissful state of detachment during the mindfulness program." But the inner strength it builds breeds objectivity, resilience, and maturity. Kids need the sense that they are building their own set of values and their ability to act from those values. Mindfulness erases the blackboard so kids can write afresh. When mindfulness is coupled with contextual seeing, then kids can not only write afresh, they can write from a new vantage point, one that is more inclusive. And that brings entirely new insights and also relief.

"Over the past couple of weeks I've been going through a lot. Mindfulness made things slightly easier. I'd rather not go into

detail, but it gave me moments where I could forget; made becoming myself again more possible."

"There are a lot of emotions I'm not sure how to handle and situations that I wouldn't know how to solve. Meditation has given me insight on how to solve those situations using a clear and level mind. Plus, it allows me to be soothed. At night I feel more in touch with myself, making it easier for me to sleep."

"I began to understand how meditation was not just sitting and closing your eyes. It is a way to explore the deep realms of the brain. It dawned on me that it was a method to get to know oneself better."

As we saw earlier, in Australian aboriginal tribes, the people talk about dreamtime. Their culture cannot be separated from this perception of the past, present, and future as all merged and available as one. There are contemporary astro- and theoretical physicists who also posit time and distance this way. Believe it or not, highly reputable theoreticians see space and time as collapsed and relative with multiple possibilities available at once. Quantum physics now postulates that more than one state or reality can occur at any one time. The science of it is as fantastical as an Isaac Asimov novel. We grew up learning that no two objects can occupy the same space at the same time. Now our scientists are unlearning this, wondering if that is only one way of understanding the reality around us. I grew up learning about adventurous thinkers who were willing to consider options that only appeared in my *Star Trek* episodes of the seventies. Newtonian physics saw the world in these concrete, linear sequences. The physics of relativity saw bends and effects of everything on everything else. From the First People's view of a single time to Nobel laureates' new speculations on the relative nature of time, can we become willing to recognize that our current view of the world is not the final or only valid one? Can we then loosen up our grip on reality as we are currently aware of it and allow for ways of being in the world that color entirely outside the lines? This is the value of holding what we see in context.

Stretching our own limits this way, we create conscious classrooms, spaces for learning that are open-ended and curious. We model for our students how wondrous and far-reaching discovery can be. As educators, we are sculpting the icons of our future in each classroom we teach. We are shaping the way the next generation grows to think about possibility—for themselves, for the world, for our interpretation of reality itself. We are shaping the value set of the world's next stewards of the possible. Teaching, in any format, is a momentous undertaking. I believe it most rightly begins with our own consideration of the fundamental worldviews we hold and our questioning of the reasons why we hold them. Our ability to do so will, in subtle but significant ways, determine how free we allow our children to be and how much trust we impart to them. That degree of freedom and trust will, in large part, determine how much confidence they have in themselves and how widely they feel they can roam the uncharted terrain of the possible.

For those who work in inner city schools like I do, we are faced daily with a level of inhumanity that, as our species evolves, I have to believe we will look back upon and consider as barbaric as the iron maidens of the Middle Ages. And we're faced with an increasing level of civic dysfunction. The roads and railways, bridges and airports of the United States are starting to look more and more like the decaying infrastructure of one of the developing worlds that have not yet grown out of feudal poverty. Our immediate concerns go to issues that we assume we could solve if we had but the moral inclination to do so as a whole. Freeing children from the shackles of poverty, discrimination, violence, hunger, depression, and fear is essential, but it is not an end goal. These steps are foundational, like the first porridge an infant eats before she grows, but porridge is hardly the meal we yearn for as an adult. As an adult species, simply taking care of basic needs is not the goal that satiates our human curiosity and desire to create a world of beauty. We are drawn towards a sense of the possible, and we rejoice when we begin to pull that possibility from the imaginal into the present. Whether it is the possible of profound human compassion or the possible of unprecedented beauty or the possible of harmony and plenty, or the possible of new communication, communion, and connection, these are the mysterious aspirations the human heart reaches for.

Footprints across Time

Every culture has an origin myth. And every ethnic group, neighborhood, spiritual community, activist sector, Facebook group, family, marriage, and even self has an origin myth. It is a story we believe that makes sense to us and answers the questions: How did we get here? What is the propulsion leading us forward? What lens defines the outlook we take on the world? Is it large enough to see what needs to be seen so we can make sense of it all?

We tend to see what we are looking for, or at least we see objects that fit into a particular set of conditions that we expect to be there. There have been some mind-bending experiments done on visual processing. In one popular format, participants were asked to watch a short film of people passing a basketball and to indicate, by pressing a button, each time a particular team had possession of the ball. So intent were they on that particular task, half the participants never even noticed a woman in a gorilla suit walk across the middle of the court during the game.[67] That is the power of our focus, our beliefs, and our unconscious assumptions. Our expectations really do shape what we see to an extraordinary degree.

Our origin stories come out of our worldviews, and they shape what we see and don't see, what is allowable, acceptable, and possible. By origin stories I don't just mean creation myths but also our fundamental ideas about how our culture came to develop in the ways it has. Our origin stories, for better or for worse, root us in the ground, embed us in the culture we come out of. They give us stability and a sense of home. Origin stories must be grand enough to allow for the first steps we as a people take; they also must be simple enough to pollinate generation after generation. If our origin stories include a personal story, it must be compelling enough to stay with us as we move from one stage in our lives to the next, from one set of circumstances to the other.

We don't usually question these narratives, just as we don't usually question the existing paradigm through which we see and touch the world and others around us. But, once we begin to unpack our embeddedness in culture, we also begin to unpack the origin story that has served as the North Star of our lives. Unpacking our basic ideas of how and why we have developed the customs, lifestyles, and values we have enables us to make room for an alternative view, a shift that may seem imperceptibly small, but is vast and far-reaching. And when we work with adolescents, as much as we endeavor to give them signposts to point the way and staffs to steady their journey into adulthood, we also want to whet their appetite with the lure of adventure, entice them with the great beyond, and tempt them to reach for that which lies past our customary way of seeing, our customary view of the world. We start to invite them to look beyond their origin stories, whether it is "I'm black," "I'm poor," "I'm smart," "I'm talented," or "I'm victimized," to something they haven't even begun to consider: "I am stardust," quite literally—all of the matter in our bodies and the air we breathe that keeps us alive has its origins in atoms and molecules formed by ancient stars.[68] Considering this makes ideas like, "I am a leader," "I have purpose," and "I am kind" seem much closer at hand.

There are positive reasons to be uprooted from our native origin stories. Sometimes we are uprooted by being presented with an alternative narrative so far out and different from our own the story we have been accustomed to turns a page, or at least folds back a dog-ear large enough to see a new tale underneath. When a sheltered suburban housewife[69] discovers the expansion of hypnosis and altered consciousness in the 1950s, when a creationist stumbles upon paleontological artifacts, when a meditator glimpses wholeness, they experience interruptions powerful enough to change or cause them to question their overarching worldview.

For many of the children I work with, their origin stories have been so disrupted by violence or absence that they lack any coherent narrative to anchor themselves. That has consequences on their stability, sense of safety, and even generosity of spirit. If we experience a shock or a trauma, a violent uprooting from our origin stories or our native myths into a reality far from our own, it creates disassociation. Some are able to rise in that disruption with more creative insights. Many aren't fully able to transcend or integrate the disruption and never quite find their mooring. These are factors educators work with in any given classroom in an urban setting. They arise from conditions we can't ameliorate, but we can support the students with mindfulness practices to re-connect with themselves, their memories, their positive inner sensitivities. This helps them integrate and create new connections, stories, and relationships.

Creating space for new roots is essential. Generations never really recover unless they are able to process and reconstruct. The privacy of shared contemplative practice gives support without attempting to re-write a new story that will have to emerge from an open heart. Guiding students through contemplative practices requires educators to hold space, let things be, and entrust students with the confidence and responsibility to find their way.

Consider the long-term effects when free roaming or agricultural African tribesmen and women were captured and taken as slaves, when Native Americans were stolen and put into Christian mission schools, when Syrian students fled from the bombing of their cities and went from high schools and colleges into acre after acre of plastic refugee tents. Those disruptors separate individuals from our cultural history, family custom, and lineage. They are seismic shifts that can't be rebuilt. Those shifts can propel an individual into an era of discovery or the cataclysms of despair. They can fashion us like blades tempered with strength and wisdom, or they can leave us disjointed and weakened by a splitting from that which gives us life. When we are in urban classrooms filled with students from a wide variety of backgrounds, whose grandparents spoke a different language, knew a different dress and custom, our ability to connect students in universal aspects of our humanity—breath, body sensation, awareness—without imposing, has a powerfully reinforcing influence. It helps students trust themselves and find their way. The important factor is allowing for difference.

In contemplative practice, it's clear how even the cues we give for paying attention create grooves that can link a child to her own experience or disconnect her. Allowing students to find their way is an essential part of empowering them to settle into the origin stories and ways of being that really are more authentic to their experience.

Usually in class when we do mindful breathing, I guide the students to rest their attention gently on the inhalation and exhalation. "Without effort or force, let your attention follow the air going in and the air going out. Notice any thoughts that arise in your mind's eye, without sticking to them. Let them appear and fade away as you keep your attention on your breath. If you don't notice any thoughts, that is fine; enjoy the space and the rhythm and sensation of the breath."

The instructions seem innocuous enough, guiding the students to notice thoughts. This helps them become self-aware and discover habits and tendencies of mind. Some of those habits are constructive and some destructive. When they become aware of critical or self-negating patterns of thought, they can learn to disregard them. When they discover positive habits of thought, they can cultivate them. I hadn't realized until this day my own bias on "thought" as the predominant object that may arise in our consciousness as we become aware.

"Excuse me miss." One girl shot her hand up after the meditation. "I don't think in 'thoughts.'"

"What do you mean?"

"When I get still, I don't have any thoughts."

"That's not uncommon; no need to insist that thoughts be there. Simply enjoy the space, and use the breath as an anchor."

"Is it normal though to have color instead of thoughts? I never knew it before, but I think in color."

"Can you describe what you mean?" We all see colors even with our eyes closed; for example, when we face a window then face a dark corner of the room. It feels like the light flickers under our lids until we readjust. But this wasn't what she was describing.

"Sometimes I see yellow then blue then oranges. It's like big shapes of color in my head that have feeling."

Other students started to chime in, trying to "fix" her experience to make it more like theirs. The way she described her "thinking" or experiencing of thought, memory, or sensation, I could tell it was different, a visual sense that was different than my cognitively biased orientation.

"At first I thought everyone saw things this way. Then I thought there was something wrong with me, so I never said anything anymore," she offered.

"I imagine many artists might experience their minds that way," I said. "And maybe some people experience sounds in a similar way. Let your experience be as it is. Explore it, become familiar with it. Allow it to enrich you and reveal things to you. When I talk about thoughts in this way, hold that description lightly and explore what arises in your awareness as it is, and see what happens."

These experiences of allowing without enforcing, of leaving conclusions open and letting students find their way, form habits for students. They model for them how to be in the world in a way that is authentic to them, even revelatory, without pushing for any particular outcome. It gives students strength and confidence in themselves. For those who experience conflicting emotions about their past, their culture, their origin stories, it allows them to find the right influences and connections, untangling emotional knots in their being so they can grow strong.

Girls, Boys & Our Embeddedness in Culture

Everywhere I'm turning
Nothing seems complete
I stand up and I'm searching
For the better part of me

I hang my head from sorrow
State of humanity
I wear it on my shoulders
Gotta find the strength in me
I am a Superwoman
Yes I am
Yes she is

Even when I'm a mess
I still put on a vest
With an S on my chest
Oh yes
I'm a Superwoman

Alicia Keys
"Superwoman"

While it is powerful to recognize we clearly have preferences that come out of our cultural, ethnic, national, or gender identification—whether it is for foods, music, clothing, or physical proximity towards one another—it can be even more deeply illuminating to see habits and preferences that are imprinted on deeper levels of our psyches. Preferences that come from earlier times in culture and habits that are encoded in us create responses in our psyches whether or not we are consciously aware of them. One of the fundamental encodings is from our gender.

This is high-profile territory to explore these days when schools regularly hold assemblies for kids as young as eleven years old and present the range of gender-identification options, and what they mean. Girls or boys may present as highly liberated from traditional gender roles and behaviors, and yet experience deep insecurities and behavioral habits that are imprinted in human memory from far back in our ancient cave-person past. There is also a biological, physiological spectrum of gender, but for now I want to unpack the identity we draw from our primarily female-male gender dichotomy.

In early human history, women, because of the delicacy and length of their pregnancies, needed a great deal of protection and support to safely carry their child to term. That need for security is still encoded in women today. Even in this day and age with all our modern conveniences, an unstable home, the lack of strong protectors, or the absence of a circle of wise women can create a bed of dis-ease, fear, and self-protectiveness for women, especially women of childbearing age. Give that same adolescent girl a stable home, reliable counsel of women mentors, secure protectors who do not encroach or intrude, and all kinds of aberrant or antisocial mechanisms can recede into the background. Human beings are delicate as well as resilient creatures. Give us a secure foundation of love and freedom, and we will trust and allow the release of our higher potentials and the better aspects of our nature. Deprive us of those essentials, or deny the disturbance created when our stability is torn from the fabric of our lives, and we will bear the scars of those wounds.[70] In those circumstances, it is rare that exclusively cognitive explanations will be able to smooth over and heal our visceral memories.

When cultural critics started to elaborate on issues raised about society and gender in Susan Faludi's *Backlash* in the early nineties, some of the discussions started to lay out a case for allegedly evolutionary reasons why women compete with women. To many modern women, on one level at least, it made sense. Looked at through Darwinian evolutionary eyes, biologically, men could spread their seed easily among many. Women, once carrying offspring, could not move easily among others. Women, this interpretation of evolutionary history postulates, competed with other women in order to attract the strongest, fastest, best mate. That hypothesis seemed to make sense and might seem to explain what every middle school and high school teacher knows. When girls enter their teens, the beginning of childbearing age, they can be catty, undermining, and even emotionally cruel to one another. They can compete in the most underhanded ways, creating in-groups and out-groups. Girls' incessant beautification of themselves also fits in this narrative, the single girl wanting to attract the best mate, and drawing his attention to her amongst the crowd through adornment and dazzle.

I'm not so sure that the early history explanation is true. There are other ways to look at and interpret behaviors and rationales. There are alternative views on gender behavior that posit that women sought the seed of many mates to bond more widely and create communal protection for herself during pregnancy and for her young. Cooperation and support seems to be a more probable characterization of our early tribes. Humans are social creatures; we bond with each other and need each other. My sense is that the story of girls' competitiveness has to do more with modern culture that has been mate/power dominated, which skews behavior. I question notions that assert that humans generally or women specifically have our roots in evolutionary or biological competition. It's an outlook that comes out of a specific existing paradigm. When we look at our pre-history, that competition story may not be the most compelling premise to explain early human socialization.

In my own work with a close women's circle for over twenty-five years, as we sought to understand ourselves and through that understanding construct a narrative of women's evolutionary habits, at first the explanation of competition seemed to hold up. But then I looked more deeply and began to factor in the cultural context in which our women's discussion was taking place. Since we are always bouncing off the culture around us, when that culture is based on power and privilege and preferences men, that set of circumstances inevitably casts a strong influence on the arising interpretation of women's habits. The pressure from the dominant culture encourages an effort to appease—not challenge—the meta status quo. The result? Even those seeking to explain this unsupportive behavior find motives that blame other women for competitive behavior. Doing this de-couples men, particularly male leaders, from their responsibility for the effect of their privileged position in the power hierarchy. Having seen this at work over several decades of attempted objective exploration of cultural conditioning and evolutionary significance, the effect of the dominant culture on the seemingly objective interpretations couldn't have been more clear. While the influence of the dominant culture is little recognized, it colors many of the theories of behavior, nature, nurture, gender, ethnicity, and even race that we hold to be true. As educators, this is something to look into with interest and open-mindedness. Only through rigorous diversity explorations, switching up the context of our inquiries, will we see how skewed our own analysis can be and how the dominant culture is swaying us, even if it is swaying us in opposition or reaction to it.

This structure of influence and effect of the cultural container on the sociological, psychological, and evolutionary theories of traits and behaviors I believe holds true for any inquiry. Mindfulness and contemplative exercises encourage new interpretations of cultural effects and personal responses. They help us dis-embed enough from the environment around us that we can objectify our conditioning and objectify the expectations and the shadow of the power structure influencing us.

Back to the example of gender, we can see that if the dominant culture is male, to a large extent that will set the parameters defining our collective narrative. Look at language—men are the default human; women are the other. This background aspect of our experience and of our culture has a profound effect on girls' sense of self, their relatedness to one another, and to men. It also has a profound effect on educators' expectations, discipline, and support. Some educators will bias the underdog; some will favor the dominant. Nature and expectations cannot be separated from the lenses our culture put on our eyes from our youngest years.

So, are pubescent girls coded to compete with one another for a male's attention? Are they vying with each other for a man's seed?

Looking back evolutionarily, in the majority of species, the male is more adorned and colorful to attract the female. Since the female carries their seed, males must compete with others for the female's permission and acceptance. The female, once carrying or caring for young, needs a protector to bring food and shield the young from predators, and yet for her own support and for care for her offspring, she relies on and bonds with other females. In a pride of lions, all the lionesses wet-nurse any of the cubs.[71] For mammals, perhaps that camaraderie and communion between females is actually evolutionarily built in. In the cultural structure of First Peoples, women's circles, women's bonding, and women's sufficiency is part of the cultural fabric and ritual. So is this women's competition a relatively recent phenomenon? Is it constructed or a by-product of an industrializing civilization? In cultures that have emerged out of a tribal configuration, the unit of family is preferenced over group. In industrial cultures, self-sufficiency is encouraged over mutual thriving, which gives rise to the merchant class. More goods to sell or provide to smaller social units. When women are relegated to home spheres and men to the market, when home spheres revolve around the smaller units of nuclear rather than extended families, the scales tip towards isolation, competition, and lack of support.

For educators, this is an important self-inquiry to undergo. It is complex and rests on being able to create enough space and non-reactivity to see in context and through different lenses and objectify our biases and blind spots. Learn how this may play out in your work culture, your neighborhood, your attitude towards girls and boys. In the classroom, create spaces that allow for alternative social bonding to occur. Build communal settings, co-creative and collaborative spaces. Allow the innate seed of community to emerge and flower. Deconstructing negative cultural habits happens more easily when we create positive experiences that are the opposite, without necessarily hitting the old habits on the head. Prejudices and biases fade as we build bridges and walk across them again and again. Once positive experiences have been established, it's possible then to reflect on and deconstruct the beliefs and power structures that resulted in the negative biases. In working with adolescent girls, defusing tensions, fights, or cattiness requires delicate and confident redirection.

Using the depth and space created by mindfulness, I draw on instinctual roots of cooperation and compassion so that we are shedding the unnatural and harmful reactivity. There is power in that, and a sense of coming home for girls when they feel safe enough to drop their guard. You can almost visibly see them breathing a sigh of relief in their own skin. In high school classrooms, surprisingly, I have seen a small amount of mindfulness on the breath calm girls down and a handful of repetitions of a Love and Kindness meditation soften the ringleaders who always had a chip on their shoulders. When those girls softened, they became role models of self-containment and regulation. The shifts were touching and dramatic. From within a circle of mistrust there's no way to create bridges. Once the power dynamic one-up, one-down has been established, talking as a first step is a hard way to dial the tensions back. Each needs to put down her sword and shield. A space of silence and mindful awareness can dissolve the walls so no one is backed against them. Then we have space, new ground to move forward from.

Teens as Culture Changers

When we look at aberrant or anti-social behaviors among our teens, a deeper understanding of the worldview we hold, the forces that shape it, and the challenge it is to truly transcend our own fixed ideas is required of us all. For educators, psychologists, social workers, behavior specialists, judges, and employers, all the more so.

Enlisting students' own understanding of the worldviews that are shaping our culture helps them begin to question what feels as close as their own skin. Which of their views are a natural pushing against the dominant culture, a natural testing of limits of youth reaching for adulthood? What are the internalized frustrations that arise from their reactions to restrictions and injustice that are rampant in a culture so in need of evolution? As students learn that they can look at the world in a developmental context without becoming unmoored and more confused about their own identity, they become intrigued and engaged. While students flower under direction and support, they equally need to gain, in safe ways, a more profound sense of responsibility for their own actions and responses. One sixteen-year-old described it like this, "By using mindfulness and self-control, I was able to refrain from doing something that would probably affect me. I stepped back and realized that it wasn't worth it."

As that sense of responsibility is cultivated in them, youth experience the drive to change their behavior, the effects they set in motion, and ultimately the culture around them on their own. We usually look to change externals first and then recognize we are also part and parcel of that world and that our own beliefs, attitudes, and prejudices also need some work. We can inculcate these sensitivities in teens through patience, example, and inspiration. We change most deeply through love and understanding. We transform our tenacious conditioning when we become captivated by a more ennobling possibility, a dream and ideal worth striving for.

One of the first steps to inspire teens is to authentically begin to explore this terrain yourself. Take your own curiosity seriously. Resist the temptation to belittle or dismiss your own musings, your own interests, your own intimations of depth and possibility. As you do this, you become a culture-changer. Challenge yourself. Become an expression of a broader worldview and a more holistic paradigm. If you suffer from the effects of competition within your own sphere of relationships, spend time exploring what a more supportive, just, and aspirational worldview would be and how it would give rise to the better human qualities you would like to see. From that ground, rather than from a negative, critical deconstructionist approach, look at the warped and twisted effects of a perspective on life that is biased, limited, and separative by nature. Begin to inhabit the world you intuit; embrace that new paradigm. Changing our own paradigm and worldview is no easy matter. Changing a significant percentage of the population is even more challenging. But it can be done. The juice for teaching and learning comes when you start to fire up the engines of transformation and you feel the traction. Engaging teenagers at this level when they are first beginning to define and understand themselves within the world is extraordinarily fulfilling. That's when teaching is infused with the unknown and with purpose. This type of education gives kids the scaffolding to construct their lives in a radically different way.

One young man I taught presented mostly as the class clown. He always had a joke at the tip of his lips. He never sat still. He had no interest in exploring the nature of awareness or in looking at the content of his own mind, or in engaging in any current events. He was smart, but kept his attention on a narrow range of issues. He was distinctly disinterested in contemplative practice. He liked the tangible, ordered, practical spheres of life. I saw him after his first semester in college. He had grown up five years, it seemed. He could not stop talking about the questions and issues on his mind—racism, inequality, the preparation he had and hadn't compared to students from more privileged, white middle-class backgrounds. Huge change, huge opening. He described how he'd been relying on mindfulness practices to help him reflect on everything he was opening up to and the overwhelming emotions it sometimes stirred up. He'd learned how to sit and create space for all these social issues and the heated reactions they provoked. He used meditation to help him clear his mind and prepare for tests that were more of a challenge than he'd expected. He was succeeding, even though he'd found that his liberal arts college was much more of a leap from his honors public high school than he'd expected. The reflective tools of meditation were turning him into not just a bright young man on a certified public accountant track, but into a caring young man who was self-motivated to think deeply and engage with complexity. And most of all, he seemed happy and confident, stretched and stretching.

CHAPTER IX

Our Culture of Individuality

Every boy in this land
grows to be his own man
In this land, every girl
grows to be her own woman
Take my hand, come with me
where the children are free
Come with me, take my hand,
and we'll run
To a land where the river runs free
To a land through the green country
To a land by a shining sea
To a land where the horses run free....
And you and me are free to be you and me.

Bruce Hart, Marlo Thomas, and Friends
"Free to Be... You and Me"

How Liberating Is Free Expression?

The freedoms we gained with postmodern pluralism came with rewards, and with a price. The rewards were a breadth of social possibilities for expression, individuation, passion, profession, art, dress, food, aesthetics, communication, and so much more. The creativity led to an outburst of new genres, of mixing and melding cultures. We saw Eastern European Ashkenazi cuisine blended with South American spices, French harlequin sequins with professional business attire for newscasters, shamanism with Axial Age religions, and on and on. The thirst for individuation also became a commoditization of what was unique, odd, or risqué. The Madonna revolution in the 1980s spiked a surge in the lingerie market, in underwear worn as outerwear. Prepubescent girls felt compelled to prance around in their skivvies, revealing their bodies as part of their freedom while exposing themselves to objectifying leers and learning to devalue their positive sense of pride. For Madonna herself (see her powerful acceptance speech for Billboard's 2016 Woman of the Year award,[72] her stance was a feminist move. For her feminism and for crossing lines of respectability, she was vilified by women and men alike.

Like with the Madonna excesses, our postmodern freedoms often came with a price too exacting for most of us to feel wholeheartedly positive. Such is the messiness of cultural change. It is also the darker underbelly of the type of allowance and push for uniqueness that has stretched the reins of respectability almost to the snapping point.

The impulse toward freedom, the impulse to explore at the edges of the known is a powerful expression of our creativity. This drive is also a move towards the unique and away from arbitrary standards by which we judge each other's talent and contributions. But it is no surprise that our freedom of expression and the rise of individual agency has led to some questionable practices and had some less than wholesome impact on us as individuals and as a culture. We as a species are not that well-regulated. As cosmologist Brian Swimme describes, in the scheme of species maturity, we human beings are in our adolescence. We are more inquisitive than mature, more fascinated by trial than connected to consequence. That is a problem in our culture. It is especially a problem for our youth, who don't have adult skills to handle the effects of poor impulse control.

The tools of mindfulness and contemplative practice, which enable kids to create some inner space and see what is there without recoil, give teens a starting point. Then through a blend of paleontology, pre-modern history, developmental neurobiology, and cultural evolution, students begin to put all of this together. They gain appreciation for what it has taken to advance to the point we have. They also gain appreciation for the fact that there are downsides to this stage of culture, and we can move into the next stage through our own conscious creation of more supportive and integrated values. Culture will move on and continue to shift. We have the opportunity to influence in which ways it will go.

In working with adolescents, the challenge for parents, teachers, and mentors will always be that line between providing direction and safety—emotionally and physically—while allowing young minds to explore beyond the edges of our more tempered adult comfort zones. The most integrated and holistic way I have found to address the complex up- and downsides of postmodernity with youth is to teach them how to work with concepts that seem incongruous. We are trained to see either/or, particle/wave, gentleness/strength. That is how we make distinctions and create value hierarchies. Being able to hold paradox is the capacity to stretch ourselves and allow mutually contradictory—but true—notions to be held simultaneously. Holding paradox is becoming comfortable with a "both/and" that shouldn't work simultaneously, yet somehow is the most accurate way to define reality that we can come close to. Handling these mutually inclusive truths has practical effects. It helps teens in the heat of intense emotion that feels so true. It allows them to feel the way they do without requiring them to take action on that truth. There are other, more positive realities to respond to rather than what their feelings are telling them is so. When they learn to do this, teens say things like:

> *"Often times we focus on our flaws and things we've done wrong. Mindfulness allows you to see your problems and accept them as normal things that happen in life. Mindfulness allows you to refocus your energy towards positive things instead of the negative ones."*

> *"Through the Inner Strength mindfulness program, I have learned to manage stress and stay calm in difficult situations. I have also learned to see the positive things in negative situations. For example, when I do badly on a test, rather than getting upset and angry, I find my weaknesses and strengths that I need to work on. I enjoyed all of the mindfulness practices we did in the class, and I will be doing these practices at home."*

"Meditation has improved my focus and my ability to understand different perspectives. And it helped me communicate better with my friends and family about issues that I have. All in all, it has helped me become a better person."

Free to Be Me, Questioning Our Self-Identity

Let's look at some of the particulars of our individualistic worldview as it relates to teens, and why and how it privileges individualism. Teens are propelled to express themselves. With hair every color in the rainbow and then some, with body art and body piercings, online avatars and custom ringtones, it seems teen self-expression is reaching a new zenith.

When did the hyper-individuation of our teens begin to form? What were the causes and the climate that spawned youth who strove to express their unique selves? The cultural factors are complex, and there is no single dimension that can explain how we came to our age of individuation. Development takes all kinds of twists and turns, some shifts for the better, some for the worse. Climate and technology, language and literature, art and science, agriculture and conquest all play roles and bounce off each other contributing to the individual trends we find ourselves in the midst of. We then begin to see that how we got here is in large part the result of propulsions we couldn't see at the time for they are so large and we are so embedded in them. We may not be able to directly trace how our earliest efforts some 140,000 years ago to create art on cave walls and to form language and writing set a path in motion that mushroomed into agriculture, villages, division of labor, commerce and monetary systems, tools and technology, immense global systems, punk and rap music... in short, the rise of modernism and then the subsequent rise of the individual. But we can begin to see the larger arc of change and direction.

Seeing in context, teaching our children to see history as one long trajectory, one great confluence of movement with so many tributaries flowing in and so many currents and patterns emerging and receding, we learn to see our own time and our personal experience as merely one infinitesimally small section of a vast indivisible whole. While this may seem overwhelming, it also explains so much. It depersonalizes. Depersonalization takes the sting out of individual hurts, failures, and fears. In an age where the individual feels so adrift and so identified with their failures, successes, and victimization, a worldview that has the capacity to depersonalize all this is nothing short of a lifesaver.

To unpack this, I want to look at a recent period of time, one that we can relate to or have lived through. I want to look at the last half century, a time that gave rise to this stage of heightened individuation, this rock-solid belief in self-accomplishment, self-expression, self-creation, and self-fulfillment, which is usually set above the priority of concern for and identification with the whole. The expectation of self-fulfillment is relatively recent. That self-identity and personal opinion, which is so apparent in any blog of postmodern times, is relatively submerged in earlier works of literature behind a more collective sense of self—the village, the tribunal, the state, the religion, universal values or truths.

But let us look at not the broad, slow strokes of how our age of individuation emerged, but at what stoked its fires to the point where we hardly have two kids in a classroom with names remotely similar, where we can print our own face on our nation's postal stamp (without having accomplished anything in particular), where we can personalize books for our children and have them be the lead characters, where almost everything can be made unique for us. This rise in individuation has empowered as well as confused our teens. It has exacerbated the teen drive to seek the edges, take risks, and act out, so they assert their individual accomplishments. This occurred at the same time as our culture stopped clearly delineating what the goal of greater individuation may be. What are the higher expressions of our human nature? What are the noble virtues and accomplishments? What makes a true leader? Striving to be unique, to stand out without a noble purpose creates a sense of restlessness, aimlessness, and futility. It creates arbitrariness. It leads to a loss of values, of purpose, and of care. Standing out—for any reason, good or bad—becomes an end in itself rather than a means to accomplish a lofty purpose, to stand out for a significant reason. We see distortions of this lust for fame in the sad story of a man who committed murder and uploaded the video of it onto Facebook, saying he wanted his moment of fame.[73] When higher purpose is undefined, it leaves kids undirected. I would argue that when we do this, we also leave them uneducated. Education imparts information, but, more importantly, it imparts the ability to discern what is of value, what is of greater good. As generations go by and these highly individuated kids become adults, their arbitrary values become entrenched. Then the larger social and cultural world starts to feel like it has no mooring, as if we left all the heavy buildings of our future teetering on spongy marshland.

The "Me" generation gained its appellation through the boomer generation's exploration of our own interiors. The self-transformation and human potential movement that began in the sixties and blossomed in the seventies became overripe in the eighties.

Incessant self-focus turned rancid and by the nineties started to show up in various pathologies. Children of the Me generation became the Me Me Me generation. Joel Stein probably most iconically characterized this phenomenon in his 2013 article "Millennials: The Me Me Me Generation" for *Time* magazine.[74] From selfies to plastic surgeries, from photoshopped identities to endless obsessions with me-time, our own needs and wants reached an exalted cultural status. Aided by personal technologies and unchecked by mainstream values, what we felt, wanted, or believed took on equal value to the needs of the whole, to greater realities and facts. Seeing from "my perspective" is valuable and has also, to some degree, helped produce more empathy. Recognizing each other's unique perspectives, we have learned to walk a mile in each other's shoes. But it has also emphasized singular unique views, rather than seeking for a greater, more holistic understanding of reality. We want to learn how to identify our own perspective, the lenses of others, and still be able to see in ways that take far more into account. That is why the ability to contextualize is such a critical skill at this point in our cultural evolution.

Let's take a quick step back and look at the strands of cultural self-identity. What does it mean to identify ourselves as "selves"? That may be easiest to see when we look at an example of a recent shift in cultural habit. Take the example of one of the intentional cultural movements—that of girls' and boys' empowerment—that asserted the positive side of individuality and self-expression. This was a quiet movement that shifted cultural values in a significant way.

When I was eleven years old in the early 1970s, I auditioned for a part in my community center play. The Jewish Community Center and the YMCA in the black neighborhood were collaborating and producing the play FREE TO BE… YOU AND ME. *It felt edgy and a little scary, even though the music and story line were as sweet as can be. I sang that chorus over and over and over: "And you and me are free to be you and me…" At that age, I had no idea that the iconic musical was envisioned by none other than* THAT GIRL *Marlo Thomas of the big hat and pretty eyes, who also happens to be the daughter of a Christian Lebanese immigrant, one of the founders of* MS. MAGAZINE, *and a visionary feminist. She was warm and delightful but iron-rod firm in her principles. When NBC saw the final script, they didn't want to include the song "William Wants a Doll" because "it would make every boy in America a sissy." She said no, she would absolutely not cut it, and if they didn't want it she would go to another network. The network gave in.*[75] *She was determined to use pop stars, including a young Michael Jackson and Diana Ross, football heroes like the mountainous Rosey Grier, and a musical story line that was going to expand the emotional options for boys and girls from that generation on.*

If I'm at all representative, I can testify that watching that show on black-and-white television and learning those songs for a grade school play changed my consciousness. I grew up thinking the role models in that play were normal. These were inculcated into my nascent value structure through lyrics, images, and vignettes that showed these new possibilities as if they were already the status quo. It left a deep imprint on me that girls could grow up to be whatever they wanted to be and boys could be caring and sensitive. No one before then had dreamed of a massive football player softly strumming a guitar singing, "It's all right to cry, / crying lets the sad out

> *of you, / It's all right to cry, / it might make you feel better. / Raindrops from your eyes, / washing all the mad out of you, / raindrops from your eyes, / it might make you feel better. / It's alright to feel things, though the feelings may be strange, / feelings are such real things / though they change, and change, and change..."*
>
> *That little chink in fixed and rigid gender stereotypes would grow wider and wider over the next few decades, giving millions the possibility to express themselves in ways that allowed for greater personal integration and expression. That opening would begin to free girls and women from stultifying and demeaning roles as sex objects and domestic fixtures, roles which emerged alongside early industrialization and urbanization for a variety of complex reasons. It would begin to free boys and men from their culture-imposed sentences to emotional deserts and inner tableaus that lacked empathy, connection, and care.*

Art has always been a meme carrier for culture. From cave paintings to body art. With modern communication technology, media has become a powerful lever, creating great shifts in culture over a single generation, or faster. But while some values shift, others, particularly ones supported by a financially lucrative industry, change far more slowly. In the half century after *Free to Be... You and Me* asserted that emotion and tenderness are acceptable inner experiences for men, we are only now beginning to catch up with what I learned could be normative in 1972.

How "free to be you and me" is the freedom (or lack of structure) that our teens have? Is it genuine freedom, or is it a freedom from mores and positive structure that should be helping to guide kids through the confusing time of "growing up?" Our culture's push to individuate is so often almost completely divorced from connection. Our children find themselves adrift and alone. Under social pressure and media pressure, they create their own "club of one." Then they find themselves not even fitting into that club that they themselves created. Social critic, novelist, and psychotherapist Paul Goodman, author of *Growing Up Absurd*,[76] wrote compellingly in 1960 that a large part of an adult's role in a teen's life is to help them maintain healthy conformity.

The challenge to find one's unique voice and reject social norms can be devastating for teens. We are such fragile creatures, and teens are little able to re-balance their precarious sense of self. Christiana was a quiet girl at one of the larger public high schools in the city. Intellectually challenging, this hundred-year-old public school churns out high achievers with academic pride and strong alumnae bonds. Discipline is expected, and quiet students are the norm, not the anomaly. With roughly six hundred kids per graduating class, it is easy to go unnoticed even by dedicated teachers. On top of that, when the school board fired all counselors in the early 2010s—in a draconian measure to cope with state budget cuts and then began rehiring them, one at a time—it left kids unsupported in many ways. This large high school still has a reduced counseling staff with a ratio of 1:500. Counselors have to handle all college advisory, admissions, financial aid, testing, and any other personal, social, emotional issues. Needless to say, even a superhuman heart would have a hard time recognizing when troubling scenarios start to play out in a single child's mind.

Christiana was one of those students who had challenges that didn't present strongly enough to be noticed. One cold grey Sunday, Thanksgiving weekend, she jumped off one of the large city bridges. Not the first child from the school to do so that weekend but the second. By some miracle, the coast guard or some passing ship was able to pull her from the steely grey river, her neck, back, and arms broken from impact, her little spirit still alive. That semester, five or six more students were prevented from following suit with early hospitalization. This girl's issues were no doubt complex. But the first details that came out when classmates shared some of their knowledge of her situation with one teacher were telling. The teen had just declared herself bisexual to a disapproving family. When not at school with its more stringent dress code, she liked to dress in vampire-movie-inspired fashion: black dress with heavy eyeliner and black lipstick. I wondered how much this was a contemporary tragedy of an adolescent pushed by cultural norms to explore the edges and to be more of a renegade than she might even have been seeking herself. Without the inner skills to work with her identity questions, without the steadying tools of contemplation and perspective, and without skills to create connections to the social circles in the school she attended, she fell through the cracks. Christiana's attempt to draw outside the lines led her to an edge that she could not, on her own, pull herself back from.

The challenge of fostering positive identities for youth while allowing those identities to be uniquely emergent for each individual is great. Especially if we want to support students to define their identities in ways that are authentic to their cultural, ethnic, and racial backgrounds, true to their own unique personalities, and congruent with their own emotional barometers. Our educational system allows little time, attention, or flexibility to support that kind of self-discovery in each child.

In one class, while teaching about the adolescent compulsion to take risks, how the teen brain through its chemical secretions "tricks" youthful humans to explore and push the boundaries, one girl in an academically inclined inner-city school bemoaned the fact that she is missing out on all that risk taking. Stating emphatically, or rather overstating in teen fashion, that in her school they are so deluged by assignments they are missing their entire teenage period. Worried, she asked, "Is it bad for my brain if I skip that stage?" While of course she had no need to be alarmed, our education system, with its emphasis on discipline and academics, rarely rewards positive or academic risk. And in that, we may be missing out on one of the most effective ways to teach, inspire, and harness teen energy to achieve outcomes that are more significant, innovative, and truly contributory.

Even within an education system that has little give and little room for adventure, we still can effect change by giving youth the tools to connect with their rich inner world and to explore the uncharted territory of human consciousness. Mindfulness practices encourage us to question, observe, and listen. We become attentive to our inner experience. This learning to observe without judgment, without pre-conceived conclusions about what is acceptable and what is not, is one of the most powerful lessons mindfulness practices have to teach us. Guiding adolescents into mindful awareness teaches them to be gentle with themselves and others. They learn not to force a conclusion or experience, but rather to be with what is. They learn to allow reality to instruct and guide them. The ability to be with what is has profoundly grounding and healing effects on the psyche. It gives students the courage not to conform to peer pressure when it goes against their own boundaries and comfort zones. It gives students new insight into the way they work. It puts tools of change in their own hands. This exploration can provide enough risk and challenge to satisfy an adolescent's need to test boundaries. It also helps them discover that they are not isolated, alone, or, when it comes down to it, fundamentally different.

Making Meaning

Lady, running down to the riptide
Taken away to the dark side
I wanna be your left hand man
I love you when you're singing that song and
I got a lump in my throat 'cause
You're gonna sing the words wrong.

Vance Joy
"Riptide"

Part of the malaise in postmodern culture we are working under is our habit of deconstructing everything as an art and a talent. To excel in the academy, we are respected for our ability to pull apart and critique other's works more than for our ability to create original works of our own.[77] Meaningless art and valueless literature has risen in popularity and in value. The appreciation of postmodern art and literature is more about deconstructing—being able to critique, pull apart, poke holes in, and see from a lens that de-values the point being made—than it is about what is most positive and constructive about the creative piece.

It seems, in that light, teens are also applying their talents and creativity with no morals, meaning, or purpose. I recently saw a performance by a brilliant modern dancer. She was part of the widely respected fifty-year-old troupe Group Motion, performing at University of the Arts in Philadelphia. A young woman with an intriguing physique, powerful control, and originality of movement spun and twerked and rolled around the stage. The title of the piece, "A Ceiling Fan." The work began in the middle, ended in the middle, and had virtually no highs or lows, simply a monotonous but captivating series of circular, repetitive, brilliantly executed moves that led nowhere. I was impressed and confused. Admiring of her artistic ability and left cold by the meaninglessness. Interestingly, the piece was not even making a point about directionlessness. A ubiquitous expression of "whatever." "So random," as the postmodern idiom goes. I happened to meet her in the hallway with her instructors, Manfred Fischbeck and Brigitte Herrmann,[78] afterwards. After congratulating her, I asked if there were a symbolism to the work, wondering if I had missed the whole point. She said, "The point is anything or nothing. Whatever you want it to be." This art had no message, no intention of a narrative, and no intention of no narrative. Meaning or purpose, it seems, had become superfluous to art.

In 1957, Ayn Rand published *Atlas Shrugged*, her final novel,[79] leading her to become one of the most popular writers of her era, her work a brilliant and cold portrayal of the commerce of human relationships, the exaltation of the motive of seeking profit or fame. Her work became the moral manifesto for Wall Street and the trading fiascos that led the world to the brink of economic collapse in 2008. It pressed us to push for a quick spike in personal gain with no sense of consequence or responsibility for social disruption and upheaval that might destabilize millions of lives. That any particular economic action might deliver a fatal blow to the family and neighborhood foundations that have kept culture—and our sense of happiness, connection, and purpose—strong since pre-modern times was hardly seen as a reason to forgo profit. She was brilliant. And she came out of specific times. Times when the clusters of urban populations around the world and the mechanization of production and the speed of mass communication were changing enabled her ideas to emerge. And to stick. None of us come out of a vacuum, nor do our ideas. Emergent ideas can appear and then bounce off a culture that is not hospitable to those ideas. They can emerge out of the pressure on our systems and ourselves. Or they can emerge from vision, from internal reaching and questioning, re-evaluating why we think what we do and how a new way of perceiving a moral direction forward might look.

It takes brave and bold explorers of the heart and mind to create an incubator for new ideas. And it takes a brave and steady teacher to hold that space within the classroom. As educators, we both need to hold the reality as it is for our students to be able to see and reflect on the climate of their times and we also need to hold a space that is somewhat incubated or shielded from the pressures of the existing cultural structures. Holding both, we allow imagination to feel into a new way of being in the world. For adventurous teenagers, this is a powerful re-direction of their desire to surf on the edges, to take risks and to go against the establishment. It gives them a challenge they can't get their minds around. One that is a little frightening. But safe. One that has the potential to lead them to a better outcome that is as yet unpredictable. To a punctuated change. A nonlinear vision of the possible.

When students say to me that they don't know what to believe in, or why bother, I see the cold, mechanistic philosophies that have influenced our culture providing highways for them to travel down. When we are cut off from our roots or meaning and purposefulness, homogenized and dazzled by goals related to acquisition rather than meaning, we leave kids without living seeds in the soil of their interiors.

The week I was working on this section was a tough week in school. It was my last day at a high school in North Philadelphia, and one of the young men, a clearly smart, handsome, and mature student, was in and out of the class. Samuel, in spite of making it to his senior year in a challenging International Baccalaureate program, was failing, not even attempting to finish his final paper for the prestigious diploma he'd worked so hard for over the last four years. He didn't care about graduating. He said he wanted to be a chef, and what did it matter anyway? Too old for the discipline of a school where he felt the lack of connection with his teachers, peers, and activities. Too young to find his way in this confusing and chaotic world without mentorship. Samuel was too smart to be unaffected or let himself be shielded in a bubble of the sheltered world of youth. The lack of jobs; lost lives of so many black men in his neighborhood; no guarantee of employment, position, respect, or safety even with higher education; with a president-elect who doesn't speak to him; a system of law enforcement, housing, and wages that seems only like an uphill or rigged battle; Samuel had become hyperactive and morose. He wore a cast on his right hand.

"I broke my wrist punching the floor the other day," he told me. "I got mad."

But he's bright. When he led a mindfulness exercise for the whole class, I could see he also had sensitivity and empathy. It might have been his first positive contribution to the class the entire semester. This last day, in between cupcakes and holiday music, I asked the students to write me a paragraph about what they learned. He had his earbuds in.

"Do it for me. I want to see what you have to say," I asked.

I don't usually put myself in the center of things. I don't usually ask a child to relate directly to me in order to do something for themselves. But sometimes we have to bend ourselves and form a bridge that they can cross over to get to a shore where there's room to explore.

To my surprise, he did. He wrote that he'd been struggling with life. He had had suicidal thoughts. "Just for a moment," he wrote, but reading that word stuck in my throat. He said he'd been looking to figure out what his mental illness was. He found some purpose learning about the "history of Africa and questions I have about life."

Roots. Connection. We all come from somewhere. Our interconnectedness with the flow of history is a big part of who we are today. Stealing away or erasing our history, making it a source of shame or fear, creates deep dissociation, unmoors us from ourselves, robs society of the spice of diversity, and leaves entire generations wondering how, where, and if they fit in.

It used to be that you could proudly tell your story and the story of your grandparents in school essays. When I asked one young man where his parents were from and he said Palestine, for the next fifteen minutes he was nervous and uncomfortable, glancing around the room. Within a few short months of the start of 2017, the once vibrant American immigrant story has become a source of fear and threat.

Creating a conscious classroom calls on educators to recognize and consider the implications of these issues. In this example, to take in the reality of all the tensions around globalization, and the valid concerns from a variety of peoples. The effect on children, who are neither causes nor agitators, is part of the classroom experience in most cities and is one that educators must contend with regardless of our personal views. Fear and threat are now part of the immigrant experience in America. It affects children who cannot reason with the prejudices. Their anxieties are neither personal nor a mental illness. They are a natural outcome of the rhetoric thrown about in the public sphere. Fear of others has resulted in our culture's increasing emphasis on separation and difference, as if one group could fence off whole peoples and keep themselves safe. In a conscious classroom, I would propose instead, "Sit down and break bread together. Then ask me who is your enemy and who is your neighbor."

Building Love and relatedness is the ultimate safety. Let us build security in our shared humanity, in our connectedness, and in valuing the artifacts from the deep layers of all of our past.

CHAPTER X

An Optimistic Future

Hold
Hold on
Hold on to me
'Cause I'm a little unsteady
A little unsteady
Mama, come here
Approach, appear
Daddy, I'm alone
'Cause this house don't feel like home
If you love me, don't let go
If you love me, don't let go.

X Ambassadors
"Unsteady"

Millennials & Mentorship

One high school student wrote this surprisingly personal response to his instructor in his final essay for the teen mindfulness program:

> *I enjoyed the Inner Strength program. It's one of those things where you initially think it would be really boring but you end up learning how important it is. It's been a unique experience because we don't generally get the chance to break down and conceptualize the roots of our stresses. I really found your story interesting—how you travelled the world to learn about mindfulness. I thought your story was really intriguing and made me give you a lot of respect. I look up to you and how wise you are. I would definitely recommend this for future students!*

How we are, how we share our lives with our students matters. We can turn the most mundane or adventurous stories into meaningful examples for our students if we take the time to make the substance of life a pedagogical tool. When we're in a room filled with students who, in all their seeming disinterest, still depend on us to be role models, our stability and lightness of being really matters. If we have any doubt about it, we only have to look back at the 44th President of the United States. In his autobiography, Barack Obama talks about his point of choice, that fulcrum when his fate and destiny were teetering. In the balance, one side held the life of a drifter and the other a path that ultimately led to the Oval Office.[80] He had a mentor who cared, and the rest is history.

Teens are thirsty, even if they don't know it at first, for educators who have a decade or two or three of experience with transformational tools. So many from the generations since the sixties have done some kind of awareness work. Ever since the human potential movement made looking at ourselves, our motivations, and the qualities of our human consciousness an acceptable, even necessary thing to do, droves have flocked to workshops and bookshops, seeking self-help and ultimately wisdom. We forget that the early participants and pioneers of the consciousness-raising movement were little more than the adolescents we are talking about instructing today. When I found *Richard Hittleman's Yoga: 28 Day Exercise Plan*[81] in 1976, I was a freshman in high school, younger than most of my students now. I learned how to watch my breath and other basic mindfulness exercises. As high school wore on, these sustained me and intrigued me. I made a pact with my best friend that we would someday go to Nepal searching for the mythical Shangri-la that the band Three Dog Night sang about. Two of today's most popular mindfulness teachers, Sharon Salzberg and Jon Kabat-Zinn, were in their late teens and early twenties respectively when they began to explore the value of this approach in an American context.

In many ways, the world has shrunk since those years. With cell phones, GPS, and satellite maps, we're more connected, but there seems to be less mystery. Distance seems smaller, and time seems speeded up. We can no longer disappear in the same way to adventure, go off the grid and search for something, we're not quite sure what, but we know we're called. Most students don't have the luxury or won't take the time to spend extended months or years exploring. During the time they do take, they want to be prepared and have that time be valuable. Now that we can YouTube anything and find a how-to video to watch or download an app or fasten a Fitbit on our wrists, we all have more access to alternative tools. But how do we know which tools to use or when we need to take our inner health and growth into our own hands? Adolescents value the input of teachers who have explored, experimented, and experienced. They pay attention to first-hand accounts that can help them with their own conundrums. Teens need wisdom. They don't want to make the same mistakes. And they, like all of us, absorb inspiration. Teachers who educate for emergence inspire us with what's possible.

Whatever we, as individuals, think of our past, we are now needed and called to make the most of our experience by seeing it in the broadest context possible and with the deepest cultural and philosophical understanding. When we interpret our own experience that way, contextualizing it in cultural and biological evolutionary history, our own stories become fascinating and meaningful. It is not our experience that matters the most, but the interpretation of our experience. Whether we have walked the peaks of the Himalayas or raised children in the city, the way we understand our personal story is what inspires and illuminates what is possible for the next generation.

The way we make our experience count is through context. Understanding how to present and relate to your experience according to much deeper and broader principles of cultural movement adds a richness and dimensionality. It depersonalizes our experience and enables students to see how their struggles and alluring goals did not arise out of a vacuum. Even the most original thinkers and awakened minds arose in the context of their times, resting on the shoulders of generations and millennia before them, reaching specific heights and conclusions because of the lens, framework, and literally what was available to them at the time.

Paradoxically, our role as educators and mentors may be somewhat easier given the overwhelming options available to our teens. In need of guidance, kids may be more receptive to the right kind of support. They do respond when they are taught from authentic insight that comes from lived experience. In the age of the search engine, kids can find out almost anything they want with a few keystrokes. They can fact-check you and background-check you. But they can't put things in context yet. They can't reason their way to the deeper meaning of their intuitions or insights. They can't access the wisdom of the ages. They look to mentors to help them figure out how to weigh and assess the value of the facts at their fingertips. They want to learn how to understand events and circumstances. Real mentorship layers in meaning and illuminates connections to gross and subtle causes. One youth put into words the value of the context setting and contemplation he learned:

> *I plan to use meditation not only to help me with sports but also in all of the stressful situations that I encounter. I feel as though I will strongly benefit from mindfulness because not only do I grow from it mentally, but it helps me grow as a person. I always think to myself, "Where would I be if I didn't have meditation?" I'm pretty sure I would be stressing out for no reason, and my life would be a mess. Meditation has taught me life lessons that I would not have learned anywhere else.*

As conscious educators, we look towards the future and bring alive the way events or actions will ripple down the line. We bring to light one long process; what is being set in motion will reverberate for months, years, decades, or longer. Bringing the long-term context to life helps students understand why their experience is the way it is. It also helps them consider what they are doing, why they are doing it, and whether they truly want to continue doing so. If we lean in to this perspective ourselves and learn how to interpret our likes and dislikes in relationship to the cultural preferences and biases that we inhale from our first breath, we can impart that context setting to youth. This requires a lot from us as educators, but the most important thing is not necessarily how far we have gotten, but rather our openness to engage in this process of archaeological excavation of ourselves. It includes our willingness to be transparent to ourselves and see our own biases. We impart a way of seeing that will become youths' touchstone. When they are confused or in doubt, they will call on this systemic way of understanding to assess the conundrum they are trying to solve. Students will apply this practical and applicable perspective when needed in their own young lives.

> *"This class taught me how to step back and look at situations from an 'outside looking in' point of view."*
>
> *"I learned to look at things from multiple perspectives. When I am working on something tough, I can look at the benefits of whatever I'm working on to encourage myself to keep working on it. This way, something very boring or painful can become something fun."*
>
> *"The most interesting thing we studied is the impact of cultural change on the mindset of the society's generations. I saw that my life is hard with so many choices, but I wouldn't want to go back in time and lose what I have. This made me more patient and accepting."*

With real training in contemplation and contextual thinking, when adolescents are moved by passion to act rashly, they will be able to see that they have a choice over the momentum they want to set in motion. They will be able to pause and reconsider.

> *All the different exercises helped fortify my mindset. Whenever a situation happens that I usually get mad towards, I am able to have a clear mind on it and react accordingly. Not only that, but all the discussions on the human brain and kids' mindset helps me to understand our feelings much more easily.*

This is the kind of education and educator this next generation responds to. Conscious, kind, uncompromising when it comes to truth and consequences. A teacher who is dedicated to creating conscious classrooms has vision yet is free of the compulsion to hold the reins, cares without suffocating. Emergent education rests on this kind of perspective and this kind of teacher. I believe our future rests on it as well.

Educating for a Better Future

It's all a hidden history and mysteries
I see vividly, hysteria
Cause misery on the interior
Shit gets more scarier
I'm never in fear
Just a little inferior
in some areas
But I share wisdom with Sumerians
Somewhere we in the place

Peace means harmony
Not war and armory.
Joey Bada$$
"Save the Children"

One of my friends, a young psychologist, recently told me about the most significant mentor he has had in his field. This mentor, a highly educated African American who has dedicated his professional life as a doctor of psychology to working with urban black men, had this to say: "It's only by working with systems that any treatment makes any sense. Only by seeing the issues as arising from causes, as part of a systemic current, a flow in motion, can we begin to respond in a way that is actually helpful and gives ground for hope to the individual."

This therapist is not alone. Some psychologists working with populations that come out of American urban poverty insist that the only way to treat and support clients is systemically. Through a whole-system approach that addresses community, health, nutrition, employment options, and education; only then will remedies for uncontrolled emotions, domestic violence, substance abuse have optimal effect. Only by taking into account a normal human response to living through the fragmentation of family and cultural structures, alienation from one's roots and ancestry can some inner experiences of rage and impotence be understood and ameliorated. When a much larger and more nuanced picture is seen, then small acts of kindness, small changes to behavior can become the fulcrum tipping towards a better life. We cannot change all the causes, nor can we stop all the momentum from decades, centuries, millennia. But life is surprisingly resilient. Life reaches towards life. Life moves in the direction of the light and air and space and possibility. How could a Malala Yousafzai, shot in the head, end up interviewed before millions of viewers by John Stewart? How could the tear in the atmosphere around the polar ice cap close in twenty-five years,[82] against all predictions? How could any one of us get over heartbreak, grief, loss, injury, despair as we do? What is it that really moves us beyond? Sometimes it is from support the size of a mustard seed.

As educators, in part, we hold onto faith each time we meet our students. It is tempting when we look at all the factors stacked against us, either as individuals or as populations, to feel overwhelmed. Certainly some events have created marks that cannot be reversed. But never doubt the resilience woven into the fabric of the universe and the human heart, and the possibility of life flowering in ways surprising and beautiful. Seeing more dimensionality doesn't mean we must respond to everything at once; it simply means there is more complexity in our awareness. We are not just seeing the closest waves; we are seeing the very origin of the moons that pull the tides. That allows us to let go and let one small act contain a tsunami of love.

As creators of conscious classrooms, let us celebrate the higher potentials of our youth. Let us love with that intensity. Let us educate with that sincerity. Let us celebrate with that abandon. And let us hope with that recognition of infinite possibility, with that very audacity with which the universe first breathed our world into being.

Endnotes

Author's note: I have made every effort to base my conclusions and observations on facts shared in the public space. Any error is mine. Sources relied upon are listed here.

PREFACE

1. My husband, philosopher Jeff Carreira, insisted I define this alphabet soup of an acronym, since the definitions seem to be expanding almost every day. The acronym stands for gender identity and sexual preference, including Lesbian Gay Bisexual Transgender Questioning.

CHAPTER I

2. Impermanence is one of the three fundamental understandings of the Theravadan Buddhist philosophy. It refers to the absence of an inherent immutable nature of created objects, which are all subject to birth, death, change, or decay.

   Thera, N. (1973).*The Basic Facts of Existence, Impermanence. In The Wheel Publication No186/187*. Sri Lanka: Buddhist Publication Society.

3. Alfred North Whitehead is one of the twentieth century's great philosophers. His treatises on Process Philosophy are complex. But his emphasis on wonder and the unknowable that permeates his work points to an important foundation for education. Among the many inspirational passages, I quote these for the reader to inspire you to pursue his work in more depth.

   > *"Culture is activity of thought, and receptiveness to beauty and humane feeling. Scraps of information have nothing to do with it. A merely well informed man is the most useless bore on God's earth. What we should aim at producing is men who*

possess both culture and expert knowledge in some special direction."

~ from Aims of Education and Other Essays (1929), 1.

"Philosophy begins in wonder. And, at the end, when philosophic thought has done its best, the wonder remains. There have been added, however, some grasp of the immensity of things, some purification of emotion by understanding."

~ from Modes of Thought

Works that informed this writing include:

Whitehead, A. N. (1967, January 1). *The Aims of Education. In The Aims of Education and other essays (1-15).* New York, NY: The Free Press.

Whitehead, A. N. (1938). *Modes of Thought*; six lectures delivered in Wellesley College, Massachusetts, and two lectures in the University of Chicago (168). New York, NY: Capricorn Books

Whitehead, A. N. (1979, July 1). *Process & Reality.* New York, NY: The Free Press. 2nd Ed.

4. Change is one of the essential insights underlying a variety of schools of philosophy. Western philosophers like some of my favorites, mathematician Alfred North Whitehead, paleontologist Teilhard de Chardin, or the contemporary cosmologist Brian Swimme talk about "process," the fact that everything is in a state of movement or flow to such a degree that it is more accurate to our experience as a continuous stream rather than as in static relationship between one solid object and another. Modern science tells us no matter how long an object may endure, from mountain ranges to galaxies, they are still in a process of forming and dissolving, never staying the same even if the fluctuations are imperceptibly small. In Eastern schools of thought the principle of impermanence was laid out as one of the essential understandings of the nature of existence. It means that all temporal objects are continuously changing, arising or being born and moving through an arc of dissolution or death. From organizational development to technological advancement to stock market ups and downs, all our systems are in a process of motion. Sometimes rapid, sometimes slow, sometimes smooth, sometimes tumultuous, but never static. By whatever path we come to it, an appreciation for this state of constant flux or change in the temporal world has powerful implications on our relationship to ourselves, the world around us, and all of our experience.

5. Against the better wishes of one of my colleagues in contemplative education, I will reserve the discussion of what it requires from an individual to be able internalize worldviews that are new to us for another book. But let me mention briefly here that, as with all philosophical ideas, there are various levels of understanding. Generally, we can more easily understand a new paradigm from within, or from the perspective of the dominant paradigm we are accustomed to. New views may make sense to us on an intellectual level. But there is another level of understanding, when we shift our philosophical center of gravity and see the world differently. When this happens, and we integrate the new perspective, it changes how we relate to ourselves, others, in fact, to our entire experience. When we internalize new views, something shifts and we cannot go back. Just as once a child learns to read, letters are no longer isolated symbols, they appear as words, concepts, and ideas opening new worlds.

6. Tragically, mental illness is on the rise. It can be helpful to see the numbers not just the conclusions, for the conclusions we come to are often influenced by the solutions we feel are desirable, possible, or probable. These statistics give a sense of how deeply disturbed far too many individuals are in our culture.

   In 2009, The Centers for Disease Control and Prevention reported, "Suicide is the third leading cause of death for youth between the ages of 10 and 24, resulting in 4,513 deaths in 2008. Further, in a survey of private and public high school students,13.8 percent reported that they had seriously considered attempting suicide; 10.9 percent had made a plan for how they would attempt suicide; 6.3 percent reported that they had attempted suicide one or more times within the past year; and 1.9 percent had made a suicide attempt that resulted in an injury, poisoning, or an overdose that had to be treated by a doctor or nurse."

   Any Disorder Among Children. (n.d.). Retrieved from https://www.nimh.nih.gov/health/statistics/prevalence/any-disorder-among-children.shtml

   If we want to look at the cost of mental illness and the severity, we can see these conclusions from the National Institute of Mental Health, "Serious mental illness costs America $193.2 billion in lost earnings per year. Mood disorders, including major depression, dysthymic disorder and bipolar disorder are the third most common cause of hospitalization in the U.S. for both youth and adults aged 18–44. Individuals living with serious mental illness face an increased risk of having chronic medical conditions. Adults in the U.S. living with serious mental illness die on average 25 years earlier than others, largely due to treatable medical conditions. Suicide is the 3rd leading cause of death for people aged 10–24 and the 2nd leading cause of death for people aged 15–24."

National Institute of Mental Health. (n.d.). [Prevalence, warning signs, and tips for parents in regards to mental illness in teens and children]. *Mental Health Facts: Children & Teens.* Retrieved from https://www.nami.org/NAMI/media/NAMI-Media/Infographics/Children-MH-Facts-NAMI.pdf

Additional statistics were draws from The United States Surgeon General report on "Depression and Suicide in Children & Adolescents.

U.S. Department of Health (1999). *Mental Health: A Report of the Surgeon General.* Retrieved from https://archive.org/stream/mentalhealthrepo00unit/mentalhealthrepo00unit_djvu.txt

7. It is important for educators to appreciate the larger social forces at play in order to better understand how to support the positive growth and development in their students and to be able to empathize with the complex issues these students may be dealing with at home or in their neighborhood. Urban poverty-level African American teens are personally impacted by the high level of incarceration among young African American men. To be able to mentor and guide these youth it is not simply to stress outcomes based on the personal actions of an individual. Individuals live in a cultural context. Justice is meted out in a cultural context. Opportunities and privileges occur in a cultural context. To truly mentor, as educators we must also see the cultural blinders and biases we hold, and we must re-educate ourselves on facts we thought we knew. For further background, see the work of:

Alexander, M. (2012, January 16). *The New Jim Crow: Mass Incarceration in the Age of Colorblindness.* New York, NY: The New Press.

Leary, J. D. (2005). *Post Traumatic Slave Syndrome: America's Legacy of Enduring Injury and Healing.* Portland, OR: Uptone Press.

CHAPTER II

8. For a **Go Anywhere Toolkit** of mindfulness audio exercises see: http://www.innerstrengthfoundation.net/teens/#audio

This chart outlines the purpose of the fundamental mindfulness exercises used in the *Inner Strength System*™:

Breath
Helps Calm And Focus The Mind. Cultivates Inner Strength Over Difficult Emotions & States Of Mind.
By gently putting your attention on the breath – a universal aspect of human experience – you can create the experience of groundedness, centeredness, and ease. You also can cultivate self-knowledge, creating distance between you and your thoughts

Body Scan
Creates Relaxation & Physical Awareness
With Body Scan Meditation you intentionally relax your body, helping you de-stress. These meditations can be used at night before bed to help you sleep more easily. It also cultivates awareness of our physical experience, so we become more attune to what's happening in our bodies (and we can take care as we notice strain, injury, or tension). It also helps us be present, and feel like we're here rather than lost in daydreams, worry, or distractions.

Thought Bubble
Cultivates Self-Knowledge, Calms A Busy Or Distracted Mind, And Gives Objectivity On Thought.
With Thought Bubble meditation, you cultivate the sense of agency over your thought process. You do not have to feel like a marionette being pulled by whatever thoughts cross the screen of your mind. This meditation enables you to create space and also see more dispassionately what you habitually think about.

Seeing Freshly aka The Chocolate Meditation
Alleviates Excessive Boredom or Dullness, Cultivates Creative Sensory Observation
Taking a very familiar action and experience, and breaking it down into its smallest component parts helps illustrate the relationship between thought (intention), automatic physiological responses (salivating), emotions (desire, expectations), and action (eating). It also introduces us to the beauty and complexity of very simple acts, bringing us to greater immediacy and appreciation for life as it is. The goal of this practice is to become aware and learn to approach your experience freshly without pre-drawn conclusions. Look at your experience with curiosity and innocence. Like an intrepid explorer, head out into uncharted terrain and see what you can discover.

CHAPTER III

9. According to US National Health reports, the rate of psychological, emotional, and physical exhaustion among those who work in professions supporting others' mental health is high. We may care but at a personal cost. Finding ways to alleviate burnout, to teach self-rejuvenating habits is essential if we want to serve those in need and not create a new pool of individuals (ourselves) who are less happy. Fulfillment, joy, and balance are crucial aspects of social and cultural health.

   Morse, G., Salyers, M. P., Rollins, A. L., Monroe-DeVita, M., & Pfahler, C. (2012, September). Burnout in Mental Health Services: A Review of the Problem and Its Remediation. *Administration and policy in mental health*, 39(5), 341-352. doi: 10.1007/s10488-011-0352-1

10. These are commonly seen as the leading causes of stress: the death of a loved one, divorce, loss of a job, increase in financial obligations, getting married, moving to a new home, chronic illness or injury, emotional problems such as depression, anxiety, anger, grief, guilt, low self-esteem. When several of these causes occur together it multiplies the emotional and psychological toll. Youth in poverty overwhelmingly experience one or more of these in their own experience or secondarily in the experience of one of their immediate family.

11. Morton, T. (2013, September 23). *Hyperobjects: Philosophy and Ecology after the End of the World.* Minneapolis, MN: University of Minnesota Press.

12. There are many studies showing the increase in doctors prescribing medications for children experiencing stress, anxiety, or an inability to focus. A poignant example comes from successful comedienne and actor Sarah Silverman, when she describes her depression to interviewer Katie Couric. Silverman's parents divorced when she was six and by the time when she was thirteen her therapist put her on Xanax. Her instructions were to take one whenever she felt sad. She ended up taking four pills four times a day. This poignant self-reveal illuminates the toll unnecessarily medicating our young people takes.

   Couric, K. (2008, October 21). Sarah Silverman's *"Demented"* Comedy [Video File]. Retrieved from https://www.youtube.com/watch?v=uZlND366m-c&feature=youtu.be

CHAPTER IV

13. The *New England Journal of Medicine,* among other trade publications documents expectations and trends of a decline in life expectancy in the United States. This recent deceleration is in contrast to a slow and steady increase in life expectancy that was the result of better public health and hygiene and the discovery of ways to treat and curb infectious pandemics. During the past 30 years, the rise in life expectancy has slowed and in some subsets of the population reversed.

    Bell, F. C., & Miller, M. L. (2005, August). *Life Tables for the United States Social Security Area 1900-2100* [PDF File]. Retrieved from https://www.google.com/url?sa=t&rct=j&q=&esrc=s&source=web&cd=1&cad=rja&uact=8&ved=0ahUKEwiJg434m6_WAhUP3YMKHZn0BfgQFggoMAA&url=https%3A%2F%2Fwww.ssa.gov%2Foact%2FNOTES%2Fpdf_studies%2Fstudy120.pdf&usg=AFQjCNGMvcaxe1GZ0YZGJef4zPzvUaokTg

    Faber, J. F., & Wade, A. H. (1983, December). *Life tables For The United States: 1900-2050 Actuarial study no. 87.* Baltimore: Social Security Administration, 1982. (SSA publication no. 11-11534.) [PDF File]. Retrieved from https://www.google.com/url?sa=t&rct=j&q=&esrc=s&source=web&cd=1&cad=rja&uact=8&ved=0ahUKEwiGqPT9ma_WAhWH7oMKHeXqBxEQFggoMAA&url=https%3A%2F%2Fwww.ssa.gov%2Foact%2FNOTES%2Fpdf_studies%2Fstudy089.pdf&usg=AFQjCNHYQWEsbp-hhJSbe9vBXU9QrAbylg14

    McNeill, W.H. (1976). *Plagues and peoples.* Garden City, NY: Anchor Press.

    Olshansky, S. J., & Carnes, B. A. (1996). Prospects for extended survival: a critical review of the biological evidence. In Caselli G., Lopez, A. D. (eds). *Health and mortality among elderly populations* (39-58). Oxford, UK: Oxford University Press.

    Olshansky, S. J., Passaro, D. J., Hershow, R. C., Layden, J., Carnes, B. A., Brody, J., … Ludwig, D. S. (2005, March 17). A Potential Decline in Life Expectancy in the United States in the 21st Century. *The New England Journal of Medicine,* 352, 1138-1145. doi:10.1056/NEJMsr043743

14. J. Tankersley of *The New York Times* looks at the trend of lower earning expections of this generation as compared with their parents. Citing "the research from a group led by Stanford's Raj Chetty [Equality of

Opportunity Project], and also including economists and sociologists from Harvard and the University of California at Berkeley, estimates that only half the children born in the 1980s grew up to earn more than their parents did, after adjusting for inflation. That's a drop from 92 percent of children born in 1940."

Tankersley, J. (2016, December 8). American Dream collapsing for young adults, study says, as odds plunge that children will earn more than their parents. *The Washington Post.* Retrieved from https://www.washingtonpost.com/news/wonk/wp/2016/12/08/american-dream-collapsing-for-young-americans-study-says-finding-plunging-odds-that-children-earn-more-than-their-parents/?utm_term=.34d7fa503e3e

Chetty, R., Grusky, D., Hell, M., Hendren, N., Manduca, R., & Narang, J. (2017, April 28). The fading American dream: Trends in absolute income mobility since 1940. *Science*, 356(6336), 398-406. doi:10.1126/science.aal4617

The Equality of Opportunity Project. (n.d.). Retrieved from http://www.equality-of-opportunity.org/

Leonhardt, D. (2016, December 8). The American Dream, Quantified at Last. *The New York Times.* Retrieved from https://www.nytimes.com/2016/12/08/opinion/the-american-dream-quantified-at-last.html

15. At the Bataclan Theater in Paris on November 13, 2015, 90 people were killed in a terrorist attack.

    What happened at the Bataclan? (2015, December 9). CNN. Retrieved from http://www.bbc.com/news/world-europe-34827497

16. On April 15, 2013, terrorist bombs planted at the finish line of the Boston marathon killed three and injured several hundred.

    History.com staff. (2014). *Boston Marathon Bombings.* Retrieved from http://www.history.com/topics/boston-marathon-bombings

17. On June 17, 2015, at the Southern AME Church in Charleston, SC a young man shot and killed 9 people in Bible study.

    Ellis, R., Payne, E., Perez, E., & Ford, D. (2015, June 18). Shooting suspect in custody after Charleston church massacre.

CNN. Retrieved from http://www.cnn.com/2015/06/18/us/charleston-south-carolina-shooting/

18. On January 8, 2011, eighteen people including U.S. Representative Gabrielle Giffords were shot in a supermarket parking lot in Casas Adobes, Arizona, outside of Tucson while holding a constituent open meeting. Six died including a US District Judge and a 9 year old child.

    Lacey, M., & Herszenhorn, D. M. (2011, January 8). *The New York Times.* Retrieved from http://www.nytimes.com/2011/01/09/us/politics/09giffords.html

19. At Sandy Hook Elementary School, in Newtown, CT, 26 were killed including 20 children on December 14, 2012.

    S., Horwitz, S., & Farenthold, D. A. (2012, December 14). Sandy Hook Elementary shooting leaves 28 dead, law enforcement sources say. *Washington Post.* Retrieved from https://www.washingtonpost.com/politics/sandy-hook-elementary-school-shooting-leaves-students-staff-dead/2012/12/14/24334570-461e-11e2-8e70-e1993528222d_story.html?utm_term=.1de89f70dedd

20. On December 2, 2015, 14 people were killed and 22 others were seriously injured in a mass shooting at the San Bernardino County Department of Public Health.

    Serrano, R. A., Esquival, P., Winton, R. (2015, December 2). Authorities Identify couple who they believe killed 14 at San Bernardino holiday party. *Los Angeles Times.* Retrieved from http://www.latimes.com/local/lanow/la-me-ln-up-to-20-shot-in-san-bernardino-active-shooter-sought-20151202-story.html

21. On June 12, 2016, a 29-year-old security guard killed 49 people and wounded 53 others in a hate crime inside a gay nightclub in Orlando, Florida.

    Zambelich, A., Hurt, A., (2016, June 26). 3 Hours In Orlando: Piecing Together An Attack And Its Aftermath. *NPR.* Retrieved from http://www.npr.org/2016/06/16/482322488/orlando-shooting-what-happened-update

22. Ricard, M. (2015, June 2). *Altruism: The Power of Compassion to Change Yourself and the World.* New York, NY: Little Brown and Company.

23. The statistics on some of the extreme weather occurrences show the impact of severe conditions as they hit more dense population centers. While each number tells of innumerable stories of heartache and loss, the overall picture is of severe weather impacting the consciousness of many more lives than in recent history. These events impact those who were in the midst of the severe weather and experienced the immediate effects—the fear, injury, loss. It also impacts their friends and relatives both near and far. It affects first responders and their families, assistance organizations, and their families. There is an ever-expanding set of people who carry the trauma of climate disasters with them.

    Cook, L., & Rosenberg, E. (2015, August 28). No One Knows How Many People Died in Katrina. *U.S. News.* Retrieved from https://www.usnews.com/news/blogs/data-mine/2015/08/28/no-one-knows-how-many-people-died-in-katrina

    The economic cost will also cause hardship for decades to come. We need to rebuild and rebuilding has a cost. There are also areas of livelihood that cannot be rebuilt instantly—farms, livestock, and other economic sectors that are built over time. These also exact a psychological toll. As Zimmerman reported, *"Besides the death toll, hurricane Katrina left many people homeless as more than 800,000 housing units were destroyed or damaged in the storm. Katrina is the costliest U.S. hurricane, with estimated damage over $81 billion and costs over $160 billion (2005 US dollars)."*

    Zimmermann, K. A. (2015, August 27). Hurricane Katrina: Facts, Damage & Aftermath. *Live Science.* Retrieved from https://www.livescience.com/22522-hurricane-katrina-facts.html

    When we remember the tsunami in Japan and the damage at the Fukushima Nuclear Power Plant, few of us recall the sheer scale of destruction. The number of confirmed deaths according to Japanese National Police is 15,894 as of June 10, 2016, with more than 2500 still reported missing. Most people died by drowning. More than 120,000 buildings were destroyed, with over 1 million partially destroyed, an economic damage of approximately $199 billion dollars.

    Oskin, B. (2017, September 13). Japan Earthquake & Tsunami of 2011: Facts and Information. *Live Science.* Retrieved from https://www.livescience.com/39110-japan-2011-earthquake-tsunami-facts.html

Taylor, A. (2016, March 10). 5 Years Since the 2011 Great East Japan Earthquake. *The Atlantic*. Retrieved from https://www.theatlantic.com/photo/2016/03/5-years-since-the-2011-great-east-japan-earthquake/473211/24

In the poverty stricken country of Haiti, we saw even worse damage, the January 12, 2010, 7.0 earthquake that struck near the capital city of Port-au-Prince left 316,000 dead or missing and over 1.3 million without homes.

DesRoches, R., Comerio, M., Eberhard, M., Mooney, & W., Rix, G. J. (2010, November 22). Overview of the 2010 Haiti Earthquake [PDF File]. Retrieved from https://escweb.wr.usgs.gov/share/mooney/142.pdf

Then in Nepal, in April 2015, the Gorkha earthquake killed over 8,000 people and left massive damage that the country is still struggling to recover from.

CNN Staff. (2015, May 10). Death toll in Nepal earthquake tops 8,000. *CNN*. Retrieved from http://www.cnn.com/2015/05/10/asia/nepal-earthquake-death-toll/

24. Grossman, E. (2011, April 7). Radioactivity in the Ocean: Diluted, but Far from Harmless. *Yale Environment 360*. Retrieved from http://e360.yale.edu/features/radioactivity_in_the_ocean_diluted_but_far_from_harmless

25. Abram, D. (1996). *The Spell of the Sensuous: Perception and Language in a More-Than-Human World*. New York, NY: Pantheon Books.

26. In Philadelphia, lead poisoning rates are cited as higher than the much-publicized cases in Flint, Michigan. Lead, a highly poisonous neurotoxin was found in at least one outlet in every school tested. Children are suffering irreversible damage. As physician and former health commissioner for the City of Philadelphia, Walter Tsou explain, "Lead is a serious neurotoxin. It can infect the bones, teeth, and kidneys. In high enough doses, it can cause renal failure, and in very high doses, it can lead to a coma." Just as an example of how widespread the problem is, the District's Office of Environmental Management for tested more than 2,000 outlets and found at least one outlet in every building over the maximum allowable lead threshold of 10 parts per billion (ppb).

Windle, G. (2017, February 28). Pa. has done nothing about lead levels in schools, report says. *The Notebook*. Retrieved from http://thenotebook.org/articles/2017/02/28/pa-has-done-nothing-about-lead-levels-in-schools-report-says

Laker, B., Ruderman, W., & Purcell, D. (2016, October 30). Philly's shame: City ignores thousands of poisoned kids. *Philly.com*. Retrieved from http://www.philly.com/philly/news/Philadelphia_ignores_thousands_of_kids_poisoned_by_lead_paint.html

27. As forester and scientist Peter Wohllenben notes, "It is now an accepted fact that the root network is in charge of all chemical activity in the tree… they deliver the products of photosynthesis to the tree's fungal partners and even route warning signals to neighboring trees. But a brain? For there to be something we would recognize as a brain, neurological processes must be involved and for these, in addition to chemical messages, you need electrical impulses. And these are precisely what we can measure in the tree, and we've been able to do so since as far back as the nineteenth century."

Wohllenben, P. (2016, September 13). *The Hidden Life of Trees: What They Feel, How They Communicate-Discoveries from a Secret World.* Vancouver, CA: Greystone Books. Pp. 51, 82-83

Kump, L. R. (2011, July). The Last Great Global Warming. *Scientific American*. Retrieved from https://www.scientificamerican.com/article/the-last-great-global-warming/

Jackson, S. T. (2016, December 19). Climate Change Since The Advent of Humans. *Encyclopaedia Britannica*, 3. Retrieved from https://www.britannica.com/science/climate-change

National Centers for Environmental Information. (2017, September 18). *U.S. Climate Extremes Index (CEI): Introduction* [Data File]. Retrieved from https://www.ncdc.noaa.gov/extremes/cei/definition

28. As the UN High Commission on Human Rights reported in 2016, a catastrophic number of people have been displaced from their homes. "Nearly 1 in 100 people worldwide are now displaced from their homes, the highest share of the world's population that has been forcibly displaced since the United Nations High Commissioner for Refugees began collecting data on displaced persons in 1951. Displacement levels are higher in some regions of the world than others. For example, more than one-in-twenty people living in the Middle East

(5.6%) are displaced. Meanwhile, about one-in-sixty people living in continental Africa (1.6%) are displaced (not including Egypt, which is considered part of the Middle East). In Europe, 0.7% of the population is displaced, similar to levels following the collapse of Eastern Bloc countries in the early 1990s."

Figures at a Glance. (n.d.). Retrieved from http://www.unhcr.org/en-us/figures-at-a-glance.html

Connor, P. & Krogstad, J. M. (2016, October 5). Key facts about the world's refugees. *Pew Research Center*. Retrieved from http://www.pewresearch.org/fact-tank/2016/10/05/key-facts-about-the-worlds-refugees/

Lovgren, S. (2005, October 18). Climate Change Creating Millions of "Eco Refugees," UN Warns. *National Geographic News*. Retrieved from http://news.nationalgeographic.com/news/2005/11/1118_051118_disaster_refugee.html

29. While the effect of radiation from the Fukushima nuclear disaster so far has not been published in detail for the lay audience, interestingly the Kogi people, an indigenous culture that lives above the shores of Columbia, became concerned by their discovery of misshapen shells, which seem to be the result of radiation poisoning. The quantity of radioactive waste entering the waterways is too vast to be "cleaned up" and even if it were possible to clean the ocean waters of radioactive contamination, there is no "safe" place to dispose of it. Studies are showing signs of radiation contamination as far from Japan as the coast of British Columbia and California. This is concerning as there is currently no known way to clean up this type of contamination or to prevent it from entering the food chain and so affecting a wide range of species.

Buesseler, K. (2016, March 9). 5 years later, Fukushima radiation continues to seep into the Pacific Ocean. *PBS Newshour*. Retrieved from http://www.pbs.org/newshour/updates/fukushima-radiation-continues-to-leak-into-the-pacific-ocean/

South Atlantic Fishery Management Council. (2001, July). Retrieved from https://books.google.com/books?id=eHI5AQAAMAAJ&printsec=frontcover&source=gbs_ge_summary_r&cad=0#v=onepage&q&f=false

From tourism to humanitarians, the people of Lesbos have been extending themselves beyond the norm to care for refugees arriving on their shores. An 85-year-old grandmother and a local fisherman have been nominated for the Nobel peace prize as representatives of the island's collective response.

Amin, L. (2016, March 24). Lesbos: a Greek island in limbo over tourism, refugees - and its future. The Guardian. Retrieved from https://www.theguardian.com/travel/2016/mar/24/lesbos-greek-island-in-limbo-tourism-refugee-crisis-future

30. The number of climate refugees is estimated to increase to an unfathomable 200 million people who will be displaced by climate related changes within the next 3 decades.

    Lovgren, S. (2005, October 18). Climate Change Creating Millions of "Eco Refugees," UN Warns. *National Geographic News*. Retrieved from http://news.nationalgeographic.com/news/2005/11/1118_051118_disaster_refugee.html

31. Cheever, S. (2004). *My Name Is Bill.* New York, NY: Washington Square Books.

32. Leary, J. D. (2005). *Post Traumatic Slave Syndrome: America's Legacy of Enduring Injury and Healing.* Portland, OR: Uptone Press.

33. Lewis, F. (2017, February 4). Enslavement Timeline 1619 to 1696. *Thought Co.* Retrieved from https://www.thoughtco.com/history-of-enslavement-timeline-45398

34. Ramirez, V. (2014, April 16). 10 music collaborations that changed the world. *One.* Retrieved from https://www.one.org/us/2014/04/16/10-music-collaborations-that-changed-the-world

35. The Beginnings of Libraries: 10,000-3,000 BCE. (n.d.). Retrieved from http://eduscapes.com/history/beginnings/3000bce.htm

    Welcome to the Library of King Ashurbanipal Web Page. (n.d.). Retrieved from http://web.utk.edu/~giles/

36. Gowlett, J. A. J, (2016, May 23). The Discovery of fire by humans: a long and convoluted process. *Philosophical Transactions of the Royal Society B*, 371(1696). doi: 10.1098/rstb.2015.0164

Miller, K. (2013, December 17). Archaeologists Find Earliest Evidence of Humans Cooking With Fire. *Discover Magazine.* Retrieved from http://discovermagazine.com/2013/may/09-archaeologists-find-earliest-evidence-of-humans-cooking-with-fire

37. Gates, H. L. Jr. (Writer), Bates, M.(Director). (2017, February 27th). Empires of Gold [Television Series Episode]. In Bates, M. (Producer), *Africa's Great Civilizations.* Washington, DC: Inkwell Films, McGee Media, Kunhard't Films, & WETA (in association with Nutopia Productions)

38. In Pennsylvania oil companies pay a flat fee of only $45,000 for every well they drill. By contrast, other states often have an overall tax on gas productionwhich can be used to offset impact on the land and also fund various state needs, including education and transportation projects. A useage fee is a more common policy in other states than a low flat fee.

Cusick, M. (2013, April 4). Pennsylvania Will Get 3 Percent Less This Year in Shale Drilling Impact Fees. *State Impact.* Retrieved from https://stateimpact.npr.org/pennsylvania/2013/04/04/pennsylvania-will-get-3-percent-less-this-year-in-shale-drilling-impact-fees/

Phillips, S. (2013, June 14). Corbett Defends Impact Fee Over Severance Tax. *State Impact.* Retrieved from https://stateimpact.npr.org/pennsylvania/2013/06/14/corbett-defends-impact-fee-over-severance-tax/

39. In 2011, the Governor of Pennsylvania, Tom Corbett cut $1 billion from education budgets statwide. 35% of those cuts was made to schools in Philadelphia, even though Philadelphia educates only 12% of the state's students. While nationwide an average of 50% of the children who attend public school are poor, in Philadelphia the number is closer to 75%. Deep education cuts further impacts those students who can benefit so much from public school. Four years later, The Washington Post reported:

As Perry and Weingarten reported, "In 2011 Governor Tom Corbett cut $1 billion in public school funding. As a result of these cuts 70 percent of school districts have increased class sizes, 44 percent slashed extracurricular activities and 35 percent eliminated tutoring programs. He has maintained this cut for the past two budgets ...[which] leaves a massive funding gap that 75 percent of public schools must account for by continuing to lay off teachers and staff this coming year. Because of this gap, Philadelphia school district is $300 million short of the budget needed to maintain its current minimal programs, forcing it to lay off 3,800 persons and strip its schools of all except mandated teachers and a principal; allowing no counselors, aides, or even a secretary to answer the phone. …Recent Pennsylvania Department of Education data reveal that the low-income student on average lost 50 percent more in state funding than higher income students: $615 in spending reductions compared to $401. The disparity in cuts based on race is even more dramatic. Caucasian students lost on average only $366 per student while non-white students lost on average $728 per student, twice the amount of funding cut from the average Caucasian student. Although the restoration of $39 million to distressed school districts last year helped minority and low income students, the impact of the disproportionate cuts continues. The remaining cuts, for example, are still 188 percent greater for minority than white students."

Perry, A. M., & Weingarten, R. (2014, October 29). Gov. Tom Corbett has slashed funding for Pennsylvania's neediest students. Fixing schools means voting him out. *The Washington Post.* Retrieved from https://www.washingtonpost.com/posteverything/wp/2014/10/29/gov-tom-corbett-has-slashed-funding-for-pennsylvanias-neediest-students-fixing-schools-means-voting-him-out/?utm_term=.01acb50c2288

Brown, E. (2015, April 22). Pa. schools are the nation's most inequitable. The new governor wants to fix that. *The Washington Post.* Retrieved from https://www.washingtonpost.com/local/education/pa-schools-are-the-nations-most-inequitable-the-new-governor-wants-to-fix-that/2015/04/22/3d2f4e3e-e441-11e4-81ea-0649268f729e_story.html?utm_term=.a307e3635ffc

Brown, E. (2015, March 12). In 23 states, richer school districts get more local funding than poorer districts. *The Washington Post.* Retrieved from https://www.washingtonpost.com/news/local/wp/2015/03/12/in-23-states-richer-school-districts-get-more-local-funding-than-poorer-districts/?utm_term=.933c97d5147a

Layton, L. (2013, October 16). Study: Poor children are now the majority in American public schools in South, West. *The Washington Post.* Retrieved from https://www.washingtonpost.com/local/education/2013/10/16/34eb4984-35bb-11e3-8a0e-4e2cf80831fc_story.html?utm_term=.d783651846c9

Rothstein, R. (2010, October 14). How to fix our schools. *Economic Policy Institute.* Retrieved from http://www.epi.org/publication/ib286/

Staff. (2010, December 1). Poverty in Philadelphia and its schools: Facts and figures. *The Notebook.* Retrieved from http://thenotebook.org/articles/2010/12/01/poverty-in-philadelphia-and-its-schools-facts-and-figures

Ward, S. (2014, April). *A Strong State Commitment to Public Education, A Must Have for Pennsylvania's Children* [PDF File]. Retrieved from http://pennbpc.org/sites/pennbpc.org/files/20140429schoolreport.pdf

Yellen, J.L. (2014, October 17). Perspectives on Inequality and Opportunity from the Survey of Consumer Finances. Boston, MA: Federal Reserve System

The Public Interest Law Center reported that "Nowhere is the gap wider than in Pennsylvania, according to federal data. School districts with the highest poverty rates here receive one-third fewer state and local tax dollars, per pupil, than the most affluent districts."

Staff. New Study Shows State Cuts to Education Highly Discriminatory. (n.d.). *The Public Interest Law Center.* Retrieved from https://www.pubintlaw.org/cases-and-projects/new-study-shows-state-cuts-to-education-highly-discriminatory/

40. This passage as reported by Trymaine Lee explains the effect of state education budget cuts on schools and kids. While government budgeting is complex, schools have a real effect on our population's earning future, quality of life, and therefore cultural stability. Consider these statistics, and think about your high school and how it was staffed. *"In the summer of 2013 the School District of Philadelphia shuttered 23 schools and laid off nearly 4,000 teachers and other support staff, including every school counselor in the district, 270 in all. Last month the city borrowed $50 million to help the beleaguered district open on time and with the barest essentials. The 11th hour influx allowed the district to rehire about 1,000 laid-off employees, including about 126 school counselors..... According to the Philadelphia Federation of Teachers, no school with fewer than 600 students will be assigned a counselor. Only one counselor will be assigned to a school with 600 or more students. And only those schools with more than 1,500 students will receive more than one counselor....In Philadelphia, like many major urban cities, a vast number of students are impoverished. They arrive in school hobbled by everything*

that often accompanies poverty: violent communities, unstable homes and food insecurity. Counselors have often been the most reliable line of defense between students and the worlds around them. The counselors handled bullying and harassment. They help soothe the emotional fallout from suicides or homicides. They are college and career counselors and they manage individualized programs for special education and special needs students. And yet, about 60% of all schools in Philadelphia public schools will not have a counselor this school year."

Lee, T. (2013, September 6). 'Who is going to help me?' In Philly schools, Life without counselors. *MSNBC.* Retrieved from http://www.*MSNBC*.com/melissa-harris-perry/who-going-help-me-philly-schools

Hartman, K., & Griffiths, B. (2012, December 6). Plan Philly: Vacant School Buildings Affect Surrounding Communities. *Philadelphia Neighborhoods.* Retrieved from https://philadelphianeighborhoods.com/2012/12/06/plan-philly-vacant-school-buildings-impact-surrounding-communities/

41. As the US Department of Education reported, "Over the past three decades, between 1979–80 and 2012–13, state and local expenditures for P–12 education doubled from $258 to $534 billion, while total state and local expenditures for corrections quadrupled from $17 to $71 billion.... All states had lower expenditure growth rates for P-12 education than for corrections, and in the majority of the states, the rate of increase for corrections spending was more than 100 percentage points higher than the growth rate for education spending."

U.S. Department of Education. (2016, July 7). Report: Increases in Spending on Corrections Far Outpace Education. Retrieved from https://www.ed.gov/news/press-releases/report-increases-spending-corrections-far-outpace-education.

Teacher, Full Time [table]. (2010). Retrieved from http://webgui.phila.k12.pa.us/uploads/Ls/2d/Ls2d78B8IP7p7MsDTs5RWg/Teacher-Pay-Grades-with-Steps-Effective-9-1-2010.pdf

"GEO Group CEO George Zoley, is America's highest paid "corrections officer." Zoley, who founded GEO in 1984, oversaw its expansion into a billion-dollar corporation that almost had a college football stadium named after it. Just last year, the firm saw a 56-percent spike in profits, after adopting a strategy for drastically reducing its taxes. That success is also reflected in increasing compensation for Zoley, whose earnings spiked from $2.8 million on 2008 to almost $6 million in 2012. Other top GEO

executives also profited handsomely at annual levels of between $1.1 million and $1.5 million." Cites Myser for *CNN Money.*

Myser, Michael. (2007, March 15). The Hard Sell. *CNN Money.* Retrieved from http://money.cnn.com/magazines/business2/business2_archive/2006/12/01/8394995/index.htm

42. As Sneed reported for US News, *"Philadelphia spends more on prisons —$231 million last budget year—than it does on libraries, parks, City Council, the district attorney's office, the board of ethics, and licenses and inspections. Combined."*

Sneed, T. (2014, December 9). What Youth Incarceration Costs Taxpayers. *U.S. News.* Retrieved from https://www.usnews.com/news/blogs/data-mine/2014/12/09/what-youth-incarceration-costs-taxpayers

"Philadelphia's per-pupil price tag last school year was $12,570 - the lowest of any comparable district except Memphis, Tenn.; Tampa, Fla.; and Dallas, the Pew Charitable Trusts concluded in a report released Thursday. Detroit spent $13,419 per student, and Boston, at the top of the peer-district list, spent $18,626." Writes Graham for a Philadelphia news outlet.

Graham, K. A. (2015, January 16). Phila. district spends less per pupil than most other cities. Philly.com. Retrieved from http://www.philly.com/philly/education/20150116_Phila__district_spends_less_per_pupil_than_most_other_cities.html

Justice Policy Institute. (2009, May). *The Costs of Confinement: Why Good Juvenile Justice Policies Make Good Fiscal Sense* [PDF File]. Retrieved from http://www.justicepolicy.org/images/upload/09_05_rep_costsofconfinement_jj_ps.pdf

Otterbein, H. (2012, September 17). *Prison Costs, crowding strain Philly resources. Newsworks.* Retrieved from http://www.newsworks.org/index.php/local/philadelphia/44407-prison-costs-crowding-strain-philly-resources45

School Spending. (n.d.). Retrieved from http://www.openpagov.org/education_revenue_and_expenses.asp

CHAPTER V

43. The Khoo Teck Puat Hospital (KTPH), is the most biophilic health facility to date. The hospital's CEO, Liat Teng Lit said they wanted a

building that "when you come in here you're blood pressure and your heart rate go down, not up." It has 140 fruit trees and a community garden. It the number of bird, butterfly, and native fish species.

Beatley, T. (2011). *Biophilic cities: integrating nature into urban design and planning*. Washington, DC: Island Press.

Beatley, T. (n.d.). Hospital in a Garden by Timothy Beatley. Retrieved from http://www.arch.virginia.edu/projects/node/2523

DeWolf, C. (2017, January 3). Buildings that blend with nature: why Singapore has them in abundance and Hong Kong doesn't yet. *South China Morning Post*. Retrieved from http://www.scmp.com/lifestyle/article/2057445/buildings-blend-nature-why-singapore-has-them-abundance-and-hong-kong

Newman, P. (2013, August 13). Biophilic urbanism: a case study on singapore. *Australian Planner*, 51(1), 47-65. doi: 10.1080/07293682.2013.790832

44. Aksinit. (2012, May 17). *How Shatner Changed the World* [Video File]. Retrieved from https://www.youtube.com/watch?v=ZjlF_iSo1Og

    Brandon, J. (2015, October 29). 12 'Star Trek' Gadgets That Now Exist. *Mental Floss*. Retrieved from http://mentalfloss.com/article/31876/12-star-trek-gadgets-now-exist

45. TED. (2010, September 7). New experiments in self-teaching [Video file]. Retrieved from https://www.youtube.com/watch?v=dk60sYrU2RU&t=826s

46. The Ocean Cleanup. (n.d.). Retrieved from https://www.theoceancleanup.com/

    TEDx Talks. (2012, October 24). How the oceans can clean themselves: Boyan Slat at TEDxDelft [Video File]. Retrieved from https://www.youtube.com/watch?v=ROW9F-c0kIQ

47. Persistently Dangerous Schools. (n.d.). Retrieved from http://www.education.pa.gov/Teachers%20-%20Administrators/No%20Child%20Left%20Behind/Pages/Unsafe%20Schools/Persistently-Dangerous-Schools.aspx#tab-1

48. Lanza, R. (With Berman, B.). (2016, May 3). *Beyond Biocentrism: Rethinking Time, Space, Consciousness, and the Illusion of Death*. BenBella Books, Inc.

49. O'Toole. G. (2015, August 28). Give a Man a Fish, and You Feed Him for a Day. Teach a Man to Fish, and You Feed Him for Lifetime. *Quote Investigator*. Retrieved from https://quoteinvestigator.com/about/ https://quoteinvestigator.com/about/

50. Hidden curriculum (2014, August 26). In S. Abbott (Ed.), The glossary of education reform. Retrieved from http://edglossary.org/hidden-curriculum

51. Gould, S.J. (2007, May). *Punctuated Equilibrium*. Harvard University Press.

52. Jensen, F. E. (with Nutt, A. E.). (2016, January 26). T*he Teenage Brain: A Neuroscientist's Survival Guide to Raising Adolescents and Young Adults* (24-85). New York, NY: HarperCollins Publishers.

    Siegel, D. J. (2014, January 7). *Brainstorm: The Power and Purpose of the Teenage Brain* (66-110). New York, NY: Penguin Group.

    Siegel, D. J. (2012, April 2). *Pocket Guide to Interpersonal Neurobiology: An Integrative Handbook of the Mind*. New York, NY: W.W. Norton & Company, Inc.

53. In this passage, David Loy gives a picturesque understanding of an interconnected cosmos, "Far away in the heavenly abode of the great god Indra, there is a wonderful net that has been hung by some cunning artificer in such a manner that it stretches out infinitely in all directions. In accordance with the extravagant tastes of deities, the artificer has hung a single glittering jewel in each 'eye' of the net, and since the net itself is infinite in all dimensions, the jewels are infinite in number. There hang the jewels, glittering like stars of the first magnitude, a wonderful sight to behold. If we now arbitrarily select one of these jewels for inspection and look closely at it, we will discover that in its polished surface there are reflected all the other jewels in the net, infinite in number. Not only that, but each of the jewels reflected in this one jewel is also reflecting all the other jewels, so that there is an infinite reflecting process occurring. Indra's Net 'symbolizes a cosmos in which there is an infinitely repeated interrelationship among all the members

of the cosmos,' according to Francis Cook. Because the totality is a vast body of members each sustaining and defining all the others, 'the cosmos is, in short, a self-creating, self-maintaining, and self-defining organism.' It is also nonteleological: 'There is no theory of a beginning time, no concept of a 'creator, no question of the purpose of it all. The universe is taken as a given.' Such a universe has no hierarchy: 'There is no center, or, perhaps if there is one, it is everywhere.'"

Loy, D. (1993, July). *Indra's Postmodern Net. Philosophy East and West,* 43(3), 481-510. Retrieved from http://enlight.lib.ntu.edu.tw/FULL-TEXT/JR-PHIL/ew25326.htm

CHAPTER VI

54. Bale, L. S. (n.d.). Gregory Bateson, *Cybernetics, and the social/ Behavioral Sciences* [PDF File]. Retrieved from http://www.narberthpa.com/Bale/lsbale_dop/gbcatsbs.pdf

55. As Henry writes about her work nationally with foster children, "*Most parents do love their children and yet, for a variety of reasons, are not able to adequately parent them. Poor parenting does not equate with a lack of love: a love that is integral to children's identity development and ability to love and be loved by others.*"

    Darla L. Henry PhD, MSW The 3-5-7 *Model: Stories of Hope & Healing for Children, Youth & Families.* Pp 33-34

56. We can see the interconnectedness and exchange or influence of matter and energy, and information, in this section from pioneering scientist Arthur Young:"The self in a toroidal Universe can be both separate and connected with everything else. For example, our Sun has a large toroidal field surrounding it — the heliosphere — that is itself embedded inside a vastly larger toroidal field encompassing the Milky Way galaxy. Our Earth's magnetic field is surrounding us and is inside the Sun's field, buffering us from the direct impact of solar electromagnetic radiation. Earth's atmosphere and ocean dynamics are toroidal and are influenced by the surrounding magnetic field. Ecosystems, plants, animals, etc all exhibit torus flow dynamics and reside within and are directly influenced by (and directly influence) the Earth's atmospheric and oceanic systems. And on it goes inward into the ecosystems and organs of our bodies, the cells they're made of, and the molecules, atoms and sub-atomic particles they're made of... .In this way we can

see that there is a seamlessly dynamic exchange of energy and information (a.k.a consciousness) occurring throughout the entire cosmic experience. It is like a "stepping down" and "stepping up" from level to level wherein the balance of energy dynamics comes into coherence appropriate to each scale."

The Torus - Dynamic Flow Process (n.d.). Retrieved from http://www.cosmometry.net/the-torus---dynamic-flow-process

57. As Amir Freimann, founder of Israeli Education Spirit Movement and co-editor of two books Education, Essence and Spirit (2012, MOFET Publication) and Education, *The Human Questions* (2015, MOFET Publication) likes to explain, "in order to see the whole picture you have to step out of the frame...and stepping out of the frame is no trivial matter."

58. Gebser, J. (1985). *The Ever-Present Origin* (Barstad, N. with Mickunas, A. Trans.). Athens, OH: Ohio University Press.

    Gebser, J. (1949). *Part One: The Foundations of the Aperspectival World; A Contribution to the History of the Becoming of Consciousness.* Stuttgart, HR: Deutsche Verlags-Anstalt.

    Gebser, J. (1943). *Transformation of the West: A Breakdown of the Results of Modern Research in Physics, Biology and Psychology; Their Significance for the Present and Future.* Zürich, CH: Ullstein Verlag.

59. As you can see from the work of the Big History Project, teaching kids to think systemically and across large swaths of time is not entirely new. In spite of its clear synthesizing value, it has yet to be incorporated in a mass scale by an educational system. Below you will see several of the educational principles the Inner Strength System™ holds in common with this great project. The Big History Project describes their work this way: "By sharing the big picture and challenging middle and high school students to look at the world from many different perspectives, we hope to inspire a greater love of learning and help them better understand how we got here, where we're going, and how they fit in. BHP [Big History Project] is like nothing else. But if you had to categorize it, you could say it's a social studies course that runs on jet fuel. Co-created by teachers, students, curriculum experts, and a dedicated team of tech developers, BHP was inspired by the work of David Christian and is supported by Bill Gates. The fundamental goal is to provide a

world class, ready-for-the-classroom resource available to everyone, everywhere. For free."

"CORE BIG HISTORY PRINCIPLES include:

• Thinking across scale

What can the birth of stars tell us about early humans? How have microbes influenced our social, economic, and environmental realities of today? Learn to draw patterns and connections across different scales of time and space.

• Integrating multiple disciplines

What do you get when a chemist, an anthropologist, and a historian meet? Three very different yet equally significant views. By integrating multiple perspectives into our thinking, we come up with new questions and insights.

• Origin stories

Since the earliest humans, we've struggled to make sense of our world and understand where we come from. Big History, which presents a perspective based on modern science, is simply another attempt to answer the big questions about our beginnings.

• Thresholds

BHP views the Universe as a series of moments, called thresholds. Thresholds are points in time when exactly the right ingredients and conditions come together and result in new forms of complexity. We identify eight thresholds in Big History and they are the key milestones in our story.

• Collective learning

Humans are the only species that can pass great quantities of information from generation to generation. This is called collective learning, and it has accelerated change in communities, civilizations, and the planet as a whole.

• Making and testing claims

Today we have more information on our phones than existed in all the great libraries of Alexandria. How do we decide what information to trust? Students learn to examine their intuition and evaluate the authority, evidence, and logic of claims."

Big History Project. (n.d.). Retrieved from https://school.bighistory-project.com/bhplive

Christian, D. (n.d.). The History of the world in 18 minutes [Video File]. Retrieved from https://www.ted.com/talks/david_christian_big_history/up-next

60. Any educator working with the tools of mindful awareness is advised to train in trauma-informed care. While mindfulness tools carry the promise and potency of deep healing, integration, hope and love, they are not magic. Challenging memories, issues, psychological disorders require insight, flexibility, care, and humility on the part of the educator so boundaries are respected, professionals are brought in as needed, and above all, children are empowered to heal in their own ways, their own time.

CHAPTER VII

61. The late Edgar Mitchell, of all astronauts, perhaps best captured the sense of moral fortitude that arose in him when his perspective changed so significantly. These quotes give some direct insight into a mind and heart touched by the vast mystery of the cosmos in which we live.

> *"You develop an instant global consciousness, a people orientation, an intense dissatisfaction with the state of the world, and a compulsion to do something about it. From out there on the moon, international politics look so petty. You want to grab a politician by the scruff of the neck and drag him a quarter of a million miles out and say, 'Look at that, you son of a bitch."*

> *"The desire to live life to its fullest, to acquire more knowledge, to abandon the economic treadmill, are all typical reactions to these experiences in altered states of consciousness. The previous fear of death is typically quelled. If the individual generally remains thereafter in the existential state of awareness, the deep internal feeling of eternity is quite profound and unshakable."*

> *"Instead of an intellectual search, there was suddenly a very deep gut feeling that something was different. It occurred when looking at Earth and seeing this blue-and-white planet*

floating there, and knowing it was orbiting the Sun, seeing that Sun, seeing it set in the background of the very deep black and velvety cosmos, seeing - rather, knowing for sure - that there was a purposefullness of flow, of energy, of time, of space in the cosmos - that it was beyond man's rational ability to understand, that suddenly there was a nonrational way of understanding that had been beyond my previous experience. There seems to be more to the universe than random, chaotic, purposeless movement of a collection of molecular particles. On the return trip home, gazing through 240,000 miles of space toward the stars and the planet from which I had come, I suddenly experienced the universe as intelligent, loving, harmonious."

Mitchell, E. with Mersch C. (2012). *The Space Less Traveled: Straight Talk from Apollo 14 Astronaut Edgar Mitchell.* Fayetteville, AR: Pen-L Publishing.

Mitchell, E. (2008). *The Way of the Explorer: An Apollo Astronaut's Journey Through the Material and Mystical Worlds.* Revised ed. Franklin Lakes, NJ: New Page Books.

62. Dr. Don Beck and Ken Wilber are among the foremost thinkers who have articulated cultural development in stages or memes.

63. While there are a variety of philosophers and cultural critics who have articulated these ideas, I am grateful for the work of these individuals for expanding my thinking with their understanding of a developmental perspective: Dr. Elizabeth Debold, Dr. Don Beck, Ken Wilber, and Dr. Robert Kegan. Each has done invaluable work on cultural development, objectifying our worldviews, illuminating how humanity develops in stages in relationship to the broader cultural, economic, technological, and environmental forces around us.

64. Hagell, A. (Ed.). (2012, March 15). *Changing adolescence: Social trends and mental health.* Bristol, UK: Policy Press

Singal, J. (2016, March 13). For 80 Years, Young Americans Have Been Getting More Anxious and Depressed, and No One is Quite Sure Why. NYMAG. Retrieved from http://nymag.com/scienceofus/2016/03/for-80-years-young-americans-have-been-getting-more-anxious-and-depressed.html

Twenge, J. M. (2006, April 4). *Generation Me: Why Today's Young Americans Are More Confident,* Assertive, Entitled-and More Miserable Than Ever Before. New York, NY: Free Press

As the Nuffield Foundation reports, "*The proportion of 15/16 year olds reporting that they frequently feel anxious or depressed has doubled in the last 30 years, from 1 in 30 to 2 in 30 for boys and 1 in 10 to 2 in ten for girls. The proportion of 15/16 year olds with behaviour problems (as rated by parents) also increased, from approximately 7 per cent in 1974, to approximately 15 per cent in 1999.*"

Increased levels of anxiety and depression as teenage experience changes over time. (2012, March 14). Retrieved from http://www.nuffieldfoundation.org/news/increased-levels-anxiety-and-depression-teenage-experience-changes-over-time

65. Trinkaus, E. (2010, December 14). Late Pleistocene adult mortality patterns and modern human establishment. PNAS, 108(4), 1267-1271. doi: 10.1073/pnas.1018700108

CHAPTER VIII

66. Harari, Y. N. (2015). *Sapiens: A Brief History of Humankind.* New York, NY: HarperCollins Publishers.

Bradshaw Foundation Research Papers. (n.d.). Retrieved from http://www.bradshawfoundation.com/research_papers.php

Greshko, M. (2017, April 26). Humans in California 130,000 Years Ago? Get the Facts. *National Geographic.* Retrieved from http://news.nationalgeographic.com/2017/04/mastodons-americas-peopling-migrations-archaeology-science/

Zimmer, C. (2013, December 4). Baffling 400,000-Year-Old Clue to Human Origins. *The New York Times.* Retrieved from http://www.nytimes.com/2013/12/05/science/at-400000-years-oldest-human-dna-yet-found-raises-new-mysteries.html?mcubz=1

67. Videos. (n.d.). Retrieved from http://www.theinvisiblegorilla.com/videos.html

68. As Geiger so simply sums up the science of the formation of basic elements, "*Every ingredient in the human body is made from elements forged by stars so are all of the building blocks of your food, your bike and*

your electronics. Similarly, every rock, plant, animal, scoop of seawater and breath of air owes its existence to distant suns."

Geiger, B. (2014, February 28). We are stardust. *Science News for Students.* Retrieved from https://www.sciencenewsforstudents.org/article/we-are-stardust

69. This video shows footage from psychology experiments during the time when LSD was still legal. Sidney Cohen, researcher, interviews of an ordinary housewife after she took a dose of LSD in 1956.

    Dave Harris. (2011, January 18). Rare footage of 1950s housewife in LSD experiment.flv [Video File]. Retrieved from https://www.youtube.com/watch?v=iGf2loLAwVE

70. Kolk, B. A. V. (2014, September 25). *The Body Keeps the Score: Brain, Mind, and Body in the Healing of Trauma.* New York, NY: Penguin Books.

71. Mammal Lactation Trivia. (n.d.). Retrieved from https://www.sciencenaturally.com/node/27

CHAPTER IX

72. Billboard. (2016, December 13). Madonna's Full Acceptance Speech at Billboard Women In Music 2016 [Video File]. Retrieved from http://www.billboard.com/video/madonnas-full-acceptance-speech-at-billboard-women-in-music-2016-7624369

73. Kennedy, M. (2017, April 18). Facebook Murder Suspect Has 'Shot And Killed Himself,' Police Say. NPR. Retrieved from http://www.npr.org/sections/thetwo-way/2017/04/18/524490044/facebook-murder-suspect-has-shot-and-killed-himself-police-say

74. NYU Professor and cultural commentator Thomas de Zengotita brilliantly highlights the effect of being mediated on the millennial generation and the narcissism it produces in his groundbreaking book, Mediated.

    de Zengotita, T. (2005). *Mediated: how the Media Shapes Your World and the Way You Live in It.* New York, NY: Bloomsbury Publishing.

Stein, J. (2013, May 20). Millennials: The Me Me Me Generation. *Time*. Retrieved from http://time.com/247/millennials-the-me-me-me-generation/78

75. In her interview for the women's history makers' library Marlo Thomas describes the battles she underwent with the television network to air the ground-breaking perspectives in her musical Free to Be You & Me.

    The Free to Be TV Special Battle [Video File]. Retrieved from http://www.makers.com/moments/free-to-be-tv-special-battle

76. Goodman, P. (1962). *Growing Up Absurd: Problems of Youth in the Organized Society.* New York, NY: Vintage Books.

77. The inadvertent downside of Descarte's theories led to excessive critique and deconstruction of arguments for the sake of critique rather than for the sake of greater truth.

78. Group Motion History. (n.d.). Retrieved from https://www.groupmotion.org/history

79. Rand, A. (1999). *Atlas Shrugged: 35th Anniversary Edition.* New York, NY: Plume, Penguin Group.

    Geoghegan, T. (2012, August 17). Ayn Rand: Why is she so popular? *BBC.* Retrieved from http://www.bbc.com/news/magazine-19280545

CHAPTER X

80. In his autobiography, Barack Obama describes a period in his youth, as an African American male, where apathy set in. Like many of his friends, academics slipped, parties began, and his mother became concerned. As a black youth, this was a crucial point. Fortunately, he made some good choices, due in large part to the influence of the adults around him. Within a few short years he could see the life outcomes playing out positively or negatively depending on choices his friends made.

    Obama, B. (2004). *Dreams From My Father: A Story of Race and Inheritance* (39-47). New York, NY: Three Rivers Press.

81. Hittleman, R. (1969). *Richard Hittleman's Yoga: 28 Day Exercise Plan.* New York, NY: Bantam Books.

82. Handwerk, B. (2010, May 7). Whatever Happened to the Ozone Hole? *National Geographic.* Retrieved from http://news.nationalgeographic.com/news/2010/05/100505-science-environment-ozone-hole-25-years/

About The Author

Amy Edelstein, author, educator, and public speaker is a powerful communicator of ideas that can help us transform ourselves and the culture we live in. She is the founder and executive director of the Inner Strength Foundation, a non-profit organization that has served thousands of inner city teens with the tools of mindfulness and contextual thinking. She is also co-founder of Emergence Education, which is dedicated to bringing new ideas to the fore so that we can create a more compassionate and inspired future.

A Cornell University College Scholar, Amy has thirty-five years' experience working with contemplative practices. In recognition of her years of contemplation and work with process philosophies, she was honored by the interfaith organization OUnI as their Wisdom Chair of evolutionary spirituality. She is the author of five books including the *Inner Strength System™ Teen Mindfulness Teacher's Manual, Love, Marriage & Evolution, Great Awakenings: Radical Visions of Spiritual Love & Evolution*, and a book of poetry *We All Come From Somewhere.*

She lives in Philadelphia with her husband philosopher Jeff Carreira and spends a lot of time walking its historic streets, inspired by America's founders to think creatively and optimistically about ways to refashion our social, educational, environmental, and cultural frameworks to better support the fulfillment and well-being of all.

Contact

For training in the Inner Strength System™ and more about the work of the Inner Strength Foundation visit:

www.InnerStrengthFoundation.net
Email: info@innerstrengthfoundation.com
FB: /InnerStrengthFnd
Instagram:/ InnerStrengthFoundation

For more on Amy Edelstein visit:

www.AmyEdelstein.com
Twitter: @amyedelstein
FB: /AmyEdelstein.Educator